The Ultimate
UK Air Fryer Cookbook

365 Days Easy and Delicious Air Fryer Recipes with Coloured Pictures and Air Fryer Time Table
for Beginners and Busy People to Cook Faster and Healthier

Dawn Wicker

Legal & Disclaimer

The content and information in this book is consistent and truthful, and it has been provided for informational, educational and business purposes only.

The content and information contained in this book has been compiled from reliable sources, which are accurate based on the knowledge, belief, expertise and information of the Author. The author cannot be held liable for any omissions and/or errors.

Table of Content

Chapter 5 Fish and Seafood   29

Chapter 6 Beef, Lamb and Pork   37

Chapter 7 Starters and Snacks   46

Chapter 8 Desserts 53

Chapter 9 Fast and Easy Everyday Favorites 59

Appendix 1: Measurement Conversion Chart 64

Appendix 2: Air Fryer Time Table 65

Appendix 3: 365 Days Meal Plan 67

Appendix 4: Recipes Index 71

Introduction

There is a reason that over such a short span of time, air fryers have become so popular and the most-sought kitchen appliance; it is the oil-free and hassle-free cooking that has made the air fryers everyone's first preference for cooking a variety of food. You can cook, bake, and produce a wide range of things. Enjoy its quick cooking without having to deal with much cleanup or grease and oil! All your favourite foods can be fried in an air fryer, and to put its Hot air frying technology to best use, it is important to have all the fine recipes in hand. So here comes a cookbook with 120 flavoursome ideas to air-fry your breakfast, snacks, entrees and desserts. So let's make some crispy chips and bake all your favourite desserts. But first thing first! Let's find out a little more about air fryers.

Chapter 1 The Air Fryer Basics

What Is an Air Fryer?

A countertop convection oven that comes in different sizes is called an air fryer. Without the excess grease and oil that comes with deep-frying, it is intended to mimic the technique. The air fryer's fan pumps hot air quickly, giving food an outside coating that is crisp. Food is cooked rapidly and uniformly with air fryers because of the concentrated heat source. A few options of what you can create are as follows:

- Baked foods such as doughnuts, cookies, and cakes
- Meats like steak, chicken wings, and pork chops
- Sides like potatoes and garlic bread

Of course, you can cook a lot more than that. For more to find, you will have to check my exclusive air fryer recipes from this cookbook.

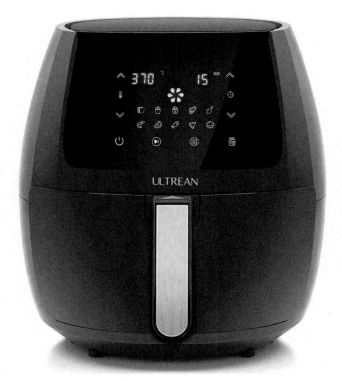

Why Do You Need an Air Fryer?

The popularity of air fryers is at its prime! All around the world, more and more people are bringing air fryer home to cook healthy, crispy and oil-free meals. These little cooking appliance has altogether revolutionised cooking technology, and now you can find the air-frying option in almost every other cooking appliance you buy. All of this is happening due to the following most amazing benefits of air fryers:

- **More Healthy**

An air fryer uses significantly less oil than a deep fryer, which is its principal health advantage. A large portion of the used oil also drains away without being absorbed by the food. As a result, you consume fewer calories and fat. These fryers' convection method encourages the Maillard reaction, a chemical process that results in browning. This has the added benefit of making the food look better while also enhancing its flavour while having less fat.

- **More Crispy Food**

Being able to generate crispy food without using oil is one of the best features of air fryers. They accomplish this by enclosing food in a perforated basket or on a rack with extremely hot air from all sides, using convection-style heating. As a result, air fryers are ideal for producing crispy French fries, onion rings, fish sticks, and other conventional fried food kinds. Because it can cover the entire surface of the meal and because the frying basket allows any excess fat to drop away, an air fryer yields crispier results than a conventional convection oven.

- **Quicker**

Air fryers cook food far more quickly than the majority of traditional alternative ways because of how they operate. The rapid frying procedure is made possible by maintaining and constantly circulating the tremendous heat generated inside

the fryer. Many versions either don't need to be heated up before use or only take a little time to do so. Compared to a conventional oven, cooking times can be reduced by more than 30 to 50 per cent, depending on the particular meal.

- **Clutter-free**

Compared to deep fryers, air fryers are much less dirty. That is because the cooking procedure only requires a small amount of oil, and it's this that makes the bulk of the mess. An air fryer may be cleaned most easily with a soft-bristle brush, dish soap, and water.

- **Safer**

Air fryers are generally safer because they are self-contained appliances and because little hot fat is used in the cooking process. Splashes and burns are less of a problem. In order to prevent the food from burning, machines are also made to turn off when the timer expires.

- **More Flexible**

An air fryer can be used to prepare most dishes that are typically cooked in a deep fryer just as well or even better. There are numerous recipes to experiment with. Surprisingly, baked items, vegetables, and steaks all performed nicely.

- **Retain Heat and Odour**

Air fryers retain heat, so unlike conventional ovens, they don't raise the temperature of your kitchen. If you reside in a smaller home or apartment, this quality is especially helpful. Due to the small amount of oil needed, there aren't any of the intense aromas that can come from deep frying.

- **Smaller in Size**

Kitchen equipment like air fryers are comparatively small; they are a little larger than toasters. They work well in spaces where size can be an issue, like a small kitchen. They may be used in an RV or camper while travelling, as well as on a campsite, thanks to their ease of portability.

- **Reasonably Priced**

Air fryers are surprisingly affordable to purchase, especially given how practical and adaptable they are. They normally cost between $50 and $150 and are offered by online sellers. However, I would advise avoiding the less expensive models and choosing quality even if it costs a bit more.

- **Simple to Use**

Most of the time, air fryers are quite simple to use and require little supervision during cooking. Simply place the food into the basket, set the timer and temperature, and let the fryer handle the rest. If you need any inspiration, there are several simple recipes available. I find frying veggies to be really simple and gratifying; the roasting effect makes the vegetables appetising.

How Do They Work?

In essence, air fryers are more intense convection ovens that are smaller and circulate hot air that has been heated by a heating element in a compact area. This heating element is located just beneath a large fan at the top, above the meal. This combination produces more intense heat in a smaller area, which cooks food more quickly than in larger, conventional ovens. Additionally, air fryers provide results that are crispier than those of an oven, making them perfect for cooking chips and other meals that require crunch.

Because of how they operate, most air fryers should be adjusted to a temperature that is 20 to 30 degrees Celsius lower than that of conventional ovens, with a 20 per cent reduction in total cooking

time. This basic instruction manual was developed based on reading items like the packet instructions for standard fan ovens. There is no need to translate anything if you are using an air fryer-specific recipe, of which there are dozens online.

Almost everything may be cooked in an air fryer; then, there are certain restrictions. Even though whole chickens can be cooked with excellent, juicy results, their smaller overall size may be a challenge

if, for instance, you wish to prepare a sizable dish of crispy wings.

How to Use an Air Fryer?

Although it could appear to be magic, air fryers have a straightforward mechanism. As you are aware, air fryers don't actually fry your food at all; rather, they cook it in hot oil. Instead, a fan that evenly distributes air throughout the appliance and high heat (from a coil near the food basket) provide a texture that is similar to that of deep-fried foods.

♦ Preheat the Air Fryer

An air fryer needs time to warm before it is ready to begin cooking, much like your oven. The majority of air fryers only require a brief warmup period, so your fryer should be ready in five minutes or less. Set the temperature of your fryer to the level at which you will be cooking (you might have a digital display or a dial to set the temperature). Some air fryers don't need to be preheated, but if you don't, your food will probably take a little longer to finish cooking. Follow the directions in your recipe for the ideal temperature to use on your fryer when you are still learning how to cook with an air fryer.

♦ Check the Dryness of Your Food

Make careful to pat your food dry before placing it in the fryer, especially if you are frying a recipe that has a marinade. Your food will be crispier when it comes out if it is drier when it goes in. Even if you believe your ingredients are dry, give them one last pat with a paper towel before placing them in the basket because too much liquid can also result in splattering and smoking. Do not use your air fryer for cooking meals with greater fat content, such as bacon. Cooking can cause the extra fat to start smoking.

♦ Sprinkle a Small Amount of Oil in the Basket

While we'd want to be able to fry without using any oil, air fryers do require a small amount of oil to make food crispy (albeit you will use a lot less than you would in a conventional fryer). Add your food to the air fryer basket after tossing it in a little bit of oil (about a tablespoon or less) to coat it evenly. You can also use a cooking spray with a high-smoke point that is manufactured with a healthier oil, such as avocado oil. Make sure the basket isn't packed too full of food. The nice part is that it won't get crispy if you do. To ensure that everything cooks evenly, it is recommended to cook in batches.

♦ **Air-Fry and Stir**

Set the time for cooking your food according to the recipe. But don't go too far! The majority of recipes instruct you to stir your food midway through cooking or to gently shake the basket. This will aid in the even cooking and excellent, crispy cooking of everything. You might also need to check the bottom tray several times while cooking foods high in fat, such as chicken wings, to remove any extra fat. Remove the air fryer base and release the basket after the cooking period has ended. After that, take your food out of the basket and wait for it to cool before eating.

Even Cooking in an Air Fryer

It is wrong to stuff your baskets too full: In an air fryer, airflow is crucial. Therefore, even while it may be tempting to fill those baskets to the brim

with fries, exercise control. A loose arrangement of the ingredients will always produce superior results, allowing the superheated convection to do its thing. Overstuffed baskets will steam rather than become crisp, and furthermore, soggy fries will not work in your favor. Do two batches in succession if you need to feed a large crowd because air fryers cook food quickly.

Packing food too tightly in the basket can limit the amount of hot air that can circulate around it and cause food to steam rather than crisp and cook unevenly. Air fryers cook food by the circulation of hot air around it. To put more food into the basket without it becoming crowded, we advise using a "jigsaw puzzle" method, chopping major proteins in half, and skewering smaller pieces of food.

Flip and Toss: Meat, poultry and seafood should be flipped midway through cooking. Although this may seem fussy, it ensures that the dish is evenly cooked. With a set of simple kitchen tongs for quick handling and to avoid reaching into a hot oven, we found it simple to accomplish this.

Toss some veggies in a bowl. Although the air fryer basket has a handle, shaking it to turn your food can result in uneven cooking. We discovered that tossing veggies, such as French fries, into a bowl midway through cooking was worthwhile since it redistributed the food much more effectively for completely equal browning. (This allows you to season the food with herbs and shredded cheese around the halfway point of cooking.)

"Lincoln log" the skewers: In addition to being enjoyable to eat, kebabs offer a simple way to distribute food in the air fryer basket. In a log cabin-style layout, stacking four or more skewers perpendicularly enhanced air exposure. Our zucchini fries were prepared using the same technique.

Oil-Mist is a Must: You will get more of a super-dried-out coating on your food if you use no oil because air fryers cook via convection, a sort of hot air cyclone if you will. You will also note right away that hard is not the same as crisp. A tiny bit of oil will do wonders, and the dish will still be healthy because it wasn't deep fried. For a thin, even coating of the chosen oil, use an oil spray bottle. For optimal crispiness, lightly spray items with oil in your air fryer before you begin cooking them and again halfway through. Note: Avoid using aerosol cans of cooking spray because the other chemicals may result in an odd, almost plastic-like coating on the air fryer's interior and moveable parts.

Extremely light objects run the risk of damaging your fryer: The amount of extremely hot air swirling around can be devastating. Therefore, use caution even though you would think that this is a perfect opportunity to make your own tortilla chips or fried wonton strips. Light things may really be pulled into the fan if your machine doesn't have a spinning tub or enclosed basket. At best, your fan or motor will be damaged, necessitating repair or replacement. In the worst-case scenario, you might create a tiny fire within an appliance containing food that has been lightly oiled, making it less flammable than deep-fried food but still very much capable of igniting.

If you are not careful, your countertop might melt: Despite being a countertop item, air fryers emit varying degrees of heat. Check the specifications on your countertop materials to determine how they manage heat and make the necessary adjustments. I place the air fryer on a rack over a sheet pan so that air can flow underneath it and any heat may be dispersed. If your counters are laminates, the glue may melt, and prolonged heat may cause other man-made materials to sear or even shatter.

*Notes to Remember: Remember that foil for the kitchen has lots of wonderful uses. In order to prevent the food from sticking to the base of the fryer basket, place the foil sheet and evenly press it into the basket. Avoid lining the basket with foil when it is hot.

You could add some water to the frying tray if the air fryer is emitting white smoke. The fryer's grease may have melted, which would explain the white smoke.

If you hear noise coming from your air fryer, do not be alarmed. This is simply the sound of the fan heating the food within the fryer.

Olive oil and other oils with low smoke points should not be used. Alternatively, if your food contains fat, make sure to cook it below the smoke point. You don't want the scent of charred food or smoking to permeate your dinnerware.

How to Clean an Air Fryer?

You will regret it if you put off cleaning. Don't let the food scraps and crumbs lie in the basket or drawer overnight; otherwise, cleaning them will be a hassle. After cooking is complete, disconnect the air fryer, let it cool, then remove the oil from the pullout drawer and discard it. When cleaning the grate, basket, and drawer after air-frying food covered in a sticky sauce, such as marinated ribs, do so while the surfaces are still warm. This will make it simpler to remove the residue.

Put the removable parts in warm, soapy water to clean them. Avoid abrasives and use a soft sponge or towel. If any of the pieces have food stuck to them, clean them after soaking them in hot water and dish soap to remove the food. Food that might be lodged in the basket or grate can be removed with a wooden skewer or toothpick. The parts should be dried individually.

A moist cloth dipped in warm, soapy water can be used to clean the interior of the air fryer. Still, the drawer and basket need to be taken out. Clean the heating element after checking for grease and food particles. Some manufacturers advise against using steel wire to remove food that has become attached to surfaces. After drying, reassemble. Dry the equipment after wiping the exterior with a moist cloth or sponge.

How Can I Get Rid of Left-over Food Odour?

Since the food is enclosed in a vessel when you are cooking in an air fryer, the odour seems to stay behind in this vessel. Even after cleaning, your air fryer may still smell strong when a food releases a strong odour when cooking. Before cleaning it once more, soak the food drawer and basket in soapy water for 30 to 60 minutes. If the fragrance still exists, cut a lemon in half, rub it over the basket and drawer, and then rewash after 30 minutes.

Be Careful with Nonstick

Customers have expressed their dissatisfaction about the nonstick coating on some air fryer parts flaking off over time on our website and in other places. Although we haven't observed this (our tests assess performance immediately out of the box), our advice for other nonstick cookware is still applicable here: Avoid using steel wool, metal utensils, or any other abrasives since they might damage the nonstick coating by scratching or chipping it. Additionally, avoid using the air fryer if the nonstick coating is peeling. Instead, make a request for a new basket over the phone from the manufacturer's customer care, or try returning the air fryer to the shop.

Conclusion

Air fryers let you cook with little hassle and more convenience. This compact and efficient appliance can be placed anywhere on your kitchen counter, and all it needs is a simple plug-in to start cooking. I have been using air fryers for the past six years, and today I cook almost every other meal of the day using them. From morning frittatas to evening muffins, cookies for kids, roasted chicken and French fries, I cook them all. And now, you can also use my extensive recipe collection and enjoy all the benefits that an air fryer has to offer.

Chapter 2 Breakfasts

Bacon Hot Dogs

Prep time: 5 minutes | Cook time: 15 minutes | Serves 4

3 brazilian sausages, cut into 3 equal pieces
9 slices bacon
1 tbsp. Italian herbs
Salt and ground black pepper, to taste

1. Preheat the air fryer to 180ºC.
2. Take each slice of bacon and wrap around each piece of sausage. Sprinkle with Italian herbs, salt and pepper.
3. Air fry the sausages in the preheated air fryer for 15 minutes.
4. Serve warm.

Sourdough Croutons

Prep time: 5 minutes | Cook time: 6 minutes | Makes 4 cups

275 g cubed sourdough bread, 2-cm cubes
1 tbsp. olive oil
1 tsp. fresh thyme leaves
¼ tsp. salt
Freshly ground black pepper, to taste

1. Combine all ingredients in a bowl.
2. Preheat the air fryer to 200ºC.
3. Toss the bread cubes into the air fryer and air fry for 6 minutes, shaking the basket once or twice while they cook.
4. Serve warm.

Kale and Potato Nuggets

Prep time: 10 minutes | Cook time: 18 minutes | Serves 4

1 tsp. extra virgin olive oil
1 clove garlic, minced
70 g kale, rinsed and chopped
280 g potatoes, boiled and mashed
30 ml milk
Salt and ground black pepper, to taste
Cooking spray

1. Preheat the air fryer to 200ºC.
2. In a skillet over medium heat, sauté the garlic in the olive oil, until it turns golden brown. Sauté with the kale for an additional 3 minutes and remove from the heat.
3. Mix the mashed potatoes, kale and garlic in a bowl. Pour in the milk and sprinkle with salt and pepper.
4. Shape the mixture into nuggets and spritz with cooking spray.
5. Put in the air fryer basket and air fry for 15 minutes, flip the nuggets halfway through cooking to make sure the nuggets fry evenly.
6. Serve immediately.

Spinach Omelet

Prep time: 10 minutes | Cook time: 10 minutes | Serves 1

1 tsp. olive oil
3 eggs
Salt and ground black pepper, to taste
1 tbsp. ricotta cheese
5 g chopped spinach
1 tbsp. chopped parsley

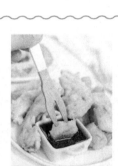

1. Grease the air fryer basket with olive oil. Preheat the air fryer to 165ºC.
2. In a bowl, beat the eggs with a fork and sprinkle salt and pepper.
3. Add the ricotta, spinach, and parsley and then transfer to the air fryer. Bake for 10 minutes or until the egg is set.
4. Serve warm.

Golden Avocado Tempura

Prep time: 5 minutes | Cook time: 10 minutes | Serves 4

60 g bread crumbs
½ tsp. salt
1 Haas avocado, pitted, peeled and sliced
Liquid from 1 can white beans

1. Preheat the air fryer to 180ºC.
2. Mix the bread crumbs and salt in a shallow bowl until well-incorporated.
3. Dip the avocado slices in the bean liquid, then into the bread crumbs.
4. Put the avocados in the air fryer, taking care not to overlap any slices, and air fry for 10 minutes, giving the basket a good shake at the halfway point.
5. Serve immediately.

Fast Coffee Donuts

Prep time: 5 minutes | Cook time: 6 minutes | Serves 6

50 g sugar
½ tsp. salt
125 g flour
1 tsp. baking powder

60 ml coffee
1 tbsp. chickpea water
1 tbsp. sunflower oil

1. In a large bowl, combine the sugar, salt, flour, and baking powder.
2. Add the coffee, aquafaba, and sunflower oil and mix until a dough is formed. Leave the dough to rest in and the refrigerator.
3. Preheat the air fryer to 205ºC.
4. Remove the dough from the fridge and divide up, kneading each section into a doughnut.
5. Put the doughnuts inside the air fryer. Air fry for 6 minutes.
6. Serve immediately.

Potatoes Lyonnaise

Prep time: 10 minutes | Cook time: 31 minutes | Serves 4

1 Vidalia onion, sliced
1 tsp. butter, melted
1 tsp. brown sugar
2 large russet potatoes (454 g in total), sliced 1-cm thick
1 tbsp. vegetable oil
Salt and freshly ground black pepper, to taste

1. Preheat the air fryer to 190ºC.
2. Toss the sliced onions, melted butter and brown sugar together in the air fryer basket. Air fry for 8 minutes, shaking the basket occasionally to help the onions cook evenly.
3. While the onions are cooking, bring a saucepan of salted water to a boil on the stovetop. Par-cook the potatoes in boiling water for 3 minutes. Drain the potatoes and pat them dry with a clean kitchen towel.
4. Add the potatoes to the onions in the air fryer basket and drizzle with vegetable oil. Toss to coat the potatoes with the oil and season with salt and freshly ground black pepper.
5. Increase the air fryer temperature to 205ºC and air fry for 20 minutes, tossing the vegetables a few times during the cooking time to help the potatoes brown evenly.
6. Season with salt and freshly ground black pepper and serve warm.

Creamy Cinnamon Rolls

Prep time: 10 minutes | Cook time: 9 minutes | Serves 8

454 g frozen bread dough, thawed
56 g butter, melted
165 g brown sugar
1½ tbsps. ground cinnamon
Cream Cheese Glaze:

113 g cream cheese, softened
2 tbsps. butter, softened
160 g icing sugar
½ tsp. vanilla extract

1. Let the bread dough come to room temperature on the counter. On a lightly floured surface, roll the dough into a 26-cm by 22-cm rectangle. Position the rectangle so the 26-cm side is facing you. Brush the melted butter all over the dough, leaving a 2-cm border uncovered along the edge farthest away from you.
2. Combine the brown sugar and cinnamon in a small bowl. Sprinkle the mixture evenly over the buttered dough, keeping the 2-cm border uncovered. Roll the dough into a log, starting with the edge closest to you. Roll the dough tightly, rolling evenly, and push out any air pockets. When you get to the uncovered edge of the dough, press the dough onto the roll to seal it together.
3. Cut the log into 8 pieces, slicing slowly with a sawing motion so you don't flatten the dough. Turn the slices on their sides and cover with a clean kitchen towel. Let the rolls sit in the warmest part of the kitchen for 1½ to 2 hours to rise.
4. To make the glaze, place the cream cheese and butter in a microwave-safe bowl. Soften the mixture in the microwave for 30 seconds at a time until it is easy to stir. Gradually add the icing sugar and stir to combine. Add the vanilla extract and whisk until smooth. Set aside.
5. When the rolls have risen, preheat the air fryer to 180ºC.
6. Transfer 4 of the rolls to the air fryer basket. Air fry for 5 minutes. Turn the rolls over and air fry for another 4 minutes. Repeat with the remaining 4 rolls.
7. Let the rolls cool for two minutes before glazing. Spread large dollops of cream cheese glaze on top of the warm cinnamon rolls, allowing some glaze to drip down the side of the rolls. Serve warm.

Simple Pesto Gnocchi

Prep time: 10 minutes | Cook time: 15 minutes | Serves 4

1 (454-g) package gnocchi
1 medium onion, chopped
3 cloves garlic, minced

1 tbsp. extra-virgin olive oil
1 (227-g) jar pesto
30 g grated Parmesan cheese

1. Preheat the air fryer to 170ºC.
2. In a large bowl combine the onion, garlic, and gnocchi, and drizzle with the olive oil. Mix thoroughly.
3. Transfer the mixture to the air fryer and air fry for 15 minutes, stirring occasionally, making sure the gnocchi become light brown and crispy.
4. Add the pesto and Parmesan cheese, and give everything a good stir before serving.

Cornflakes Toast Sticks

Prep time: 10 minutes | Cook time: 6 minutes | Serves 4

2 eggs
120 ml milk
⅛ tsp. salt
½ tsp. pure vanilla extract

30 g crushed cornflakes
6 slices sandwich bread, each slice cut into 4 strips
Maple syrup, for dipping
Cooking spray

1. Preheat the air fryer to 200ºC.
2. In a small bowl, beat together the eggs, milk, salt, and vanilla.
3. Put crushed cornflakes on a plate or in a shallow dish.
4. Dip bread strips in egg mixture, shake off excess, and roll in cornflake crumbs.
5. Spray both sides of bread strips with oil.
6. Put bread strips in air fryer basket in a single layer.
7. Air fry for 6 minutes or until golden brown.
8. Repeat steps 5 and 6 to air fry remaining French toast sticks.
9. Serve with maple syrup.

Cheesy Bacon Quiche

Prep time: 15 minutes | Cook time: 20 minutes | Serves 4

1 tbsp. olive oil
1 shortcrust pastry
3 tbsps. Greek yogurt
40 g grated Cheddar cheese
85 g chopped bacon
4 eggs, beaten

¼ tsp. garlic powder
Pinch of black pepper
¼ tsp. onion powder
¼ tsp. sea salt
Flour, for sprinkling

1. Preheat the air fryer to 165ºC.
2. Take 8 ramekins and grease with olive oil. Coat with a sprinkling of flour, tapping to remove any excess.
3. Cut the shortcrust pastry in 8 and place each piece at the bottom of each ramekin.
4. Put all the other ingredients in a bowl and combine well. Spoon equal amounts of the filling into each piece of pastry.

5. Bake the ramekins in the air fryer for 20 minutes.
6. Serve warm.

Soufflé

Prep time: 10 minutes | Cook time: 22 minutes | Serves 4

75 g butter, melted
30 g flour
240 ml milk
28 g sugar
4 egg yolks

1 tsp. vanilla extract
6 egg whites
1 tsp. cream of tartar
Cooking spray

1. In a bowl, mix the butter and flour until a smooth consistency is achieved.
2. Pour the milk into a saucepan over medium-low heat. Add the sugar and allow to dissolve before raising the heat to boil the milk.
3. Pour in the flour and butter mixture and stir rigorously for 7 minutes to eliminate any lumps. Make sure the mixture thickens. Take off the heat and allow to cool for 15 minutes.
4. Preheat the air fryer to 160ºC. Spritz 6 soufflé dishes with cooking spray.
5. Put the egg yolks and vanilla extract in a separate bowl and beat them together with a fork. Pour in the milk and combine well to incorporate everything.
6. In a smaller bowl mix the egg whites and cream of tartar with a fork. Fold into the egg yolks-milk mixture before adding in the flour mixture. Transfer equal amounts to the 6 soufflé dishes.
7. Put the dishes in the air fryer and bake for 15 minutes.
8. Serve warm.

Potato Bread Rolls

Prep time: 15 minutes | Cook time: 20 minutes | Serves 5

5 large potatoes, boiled and mashed
Salt and ground black pepper, to taste
½ tsp. mustard seeds
1 tbsp. olive oil
2 small onions, chopped

2 sprigs curry leaves
½ tsp. turmeric powder
2 green chilies, seeded and chopped
1 bunch coriander, chopped
8 slices bread, brown sides discarded

1. Preheat the air fryer to 205ºC.
2. Put the mashed potatoes in a bowl and sprinkle on salt and pepper. Set to one side.
3. Fry the mustard seeds in olive oil over a medium-low heat in a skillet, stirring continuously, until they sputter.
4. Add the onions and cook until they turn translucent. Add the curry leaves and turmeric powder and stir. Cook for a further 2 minutes until fragrant.
5. Remove the pan from the heat and combine with the potatoes. Mix in the green chilies and coriander.
6. Wet the bread slightly and drain of any excess liquid.
7. Spoon a small amount of the potato mixture into the centre of the bread and enclose the bread around the filling, sealing it entirely. Continue until the rest of the bread and filling is used up. Brush each bread roll with some oil and transfer to the basket of the air fryer.
8. Air fry for 15 minutes, gently shaking the air fryer basket at the halfway point to ensure each roll is cooked evenly.
9. Serve immediately.

Ritzy Vegetable Frittata

4 eggs
60 ml milk
Sea salt and ground black pepper, to taste
1 courgette, sliced
½ bunch asparagus, sliced
45 g mushrooms, sliced

30 g spinach, shredded
25 g red onion, sliced
½ tbsp. olive oil
5 tbsps. feta cheese, crumbled
4 tbsps. Cheddar cheese, grated
¼ bunch chives, minced

1. In a bowl, mix the eggs, milk, salt and pepper.
2. Over a medium heat, sauté the vegetables for 6 minutes with the olive oil in a nonstick pan.
3. Put some parchment paper in the base of a baking tin. Pour in the vegetables, followed by the egg mixture. Top with the feta and grated Cheddar.
4. Preheat the air fryer to 160ºC.
5. Transfer the baking tin to the air fryer and bake for 15 minutes. Remove the frittata from the air fryer and leave to cool for 5 minutes.
6. Top with the minced chives and serve.

Chapter 3 Vegetables

Balsamic Brussels Sprouts

Prep time: 5 minutes | Cook time: 13 minutes | Serves 2

170 g Brussels sprouts, halved
1 tbsp. olive oil
1 tbsp. balsamic vinegar
1 tbsp. maple syrup
¼ tsp. sea salt

1. Preheat the air fryer to 190ºC.
2. Evenly coat the Brussels sprouts with the olive oil, balsamic vinegar, maple syrup, and salt.
3. Transfer to the air fryer basket and air fry for 5 minutes. Give the basket a good shake, turn the heat to 200ºC and continue to air fry for another 8 minutes.
4. Serve hot.

Roasted Lemony Broccoli

Prep time: 5 minutes | Cook time: 15 minutes | Serves 6

2 heads broccoli, cut into florets
2 tsps. extra-virgin olive oil, plus more for coating
1 tsp. salt
½ tsp. black pepper
1 clove garlic, minced
½ tsp. lemon juice

1. Cover the air fryer basket with aluminum foil and coat with a light brushing of oil.
2. Preheat the air fryer to 190ºC.
3. In a bowl, combine all ingredients, save for the lemon juice, and transfer to the air fryer basket. Roast for 15 minutes.
4. Serve with the lemon juice.

Lush Summer Rolls

Prep time: 15 minutes | Cook time: 15 minutes | Serves 4

75 g shiitake mushroom, sliced thinly
1 celery stalk, chopped
1 medium carrot, shredded
½ tsp. finely chopped ginger
1 tsp. sugar

1 tbsp. soy sauce
1 tsp. nutritional yeast
8 spring roll sheets
1 tsp. corn flour
2 tbsps. water

1. In a bowl, combine the ginger, soy sauce, nutritional yeast, carrots, celery, mushroom, and sugar.
2. Mix the cornflour and water to create an adhesive for the spring rolls.
3. Scoop a tablespoonful of the vegetable mixture into the middle of the spring roll sheets. Brush the edges of the sheets with the cornflour adhesive and enclose around the filling to make spring rolls.
4. Preheat the air fryer to 200ºC. When warm, place the rolls inside and air fry for 15 minutes or until crisp.
5. Serve hot.

Corn Pakodas

Prep time: 10 minutes | Cook time: 8 minutes | Serves 5

125 g flour
¼ tsp. baking soda
¼ tsp. salt
½ tsp. curry powder
½ tsp. red chili powder
¼ tsp. turmeric powder
60 ml water
10 cobs baby corn, blanched
Cooking spray

1. Preheat the air fryer to 220ºC.
2. Cover the air fryer basket with aluminum foil and spritz with the cooking spray.
3. In a bowl, combine all the ingredients, save for the corn. Stir with a whisk until well combined.
4. Coat the corn in the batter and put inside the air fryer.
5. Air fry for 8 minutes until a golden brown colour is achieved.
6. Serve hot.

Super Vegetable Burger

Prep time: 15 minutes | Cook time: 12 minutes | Serves 8

227 g cauliflower, steamed and diced, rinsed and drained
2 tsps. coconut oil, melted
2 tsps. minced garlic
22 g desiccated coconut
80 g oats
3 tbsps. flour
1 tbsp. flaxseeds plus 3 tbsps. water, divided
1 tsp. mustard powder
2 tsps. thyme
2 tsps. parsley
2 tsps. chives
Salt and ground black pepper, to taste
120 g bread crumbs

1. Preheat the air fryer to 200ºC.
2. Combine the cauliflower with all the ingredients, except for the bread crumbs, incorporating everything well.
3. Using the hands, shape 8 equal-sized amounts of the mixture into burger patties. Coat the patties in bread crumbs before putting them in the air fryer basket in a single layer.
4. Air fry for 12 minutes or until crispy.
5. Serve hot.

Sriracha Golden Cauliflower

Prep time: 5 minutes | Cook time: 17 minutes | Serves 4

60 g vegan butter, melted
60 g sriracha sauce
450 g cauliflower florets

120 g bread crumbs
1 tsp. salt

1. Preheat the air fryer to 190ºC.
2. Mix the sriracha and vegan butter in a bowl and pour this mixture over the cauliflower, taking care to cover each floret entirely.
3. In a separate bowl, combine the bread crumbs and salt.
4. Dip the cauliflower florets in the bread crumbs, coating each one well. Air fry in the air fryer for 17 minutes.
5. Serve hot.

Cashew Stuffed Mushrooms

Prep time: 10 minutes | Cook time: 15 minutes | Serves 6

60 g basil
80 g cashew, soaked overnight
120 g nutritional yeast
1 tbsp. lemon juice
2 cloves garlic
1 tbsp. olive oil
Salt, to taste
454 g baby Bella mushroom, stems removed

1. Preheat the air fryer to 200ºC.
2. Prepare the pesto. In a food processor, blend the basil, cashew nuts, nutritional yeast, lemon juice, garlic and olive oil to combine well. Sprinkle with salt as desired.
3. Turn the mushrooms cap-side down and spread the pesto on the underside of each cap.
4. Transfer to the air fryer and air fry for 15 minutes.
5. Serve warm.

Fig, Chickpea, and Rocket Salad

Prep time: 15 minutes | Cook time: 20 minutes | Serves 4

8 fresh figs, halved
260 g cooked chickpeas
1 tsp. crushed roasted cumin seeds
4 tbsps. balsamic vinegar
2 tbsps. extra-virgin olive oil, plus more for greasing
Salt and ground black pepper, to taste
60 g rocket, washed and dried

1. Preheat the air fryer to 190ºC.
2. Cover the air fryer basket with aluminum foil and grease lightly with oil. Put the figs in the air fryer basket and air

fry for 10 minutes.

3. In a bowl, combine the chickpeas and cumin seeds.
4. Remove the air fried figs from the air fryer and replace with the chickpeas. Air fry for 10 minutes. Leave to cool.
5. In the meantime, prepare the dressing. Mix the balsamic vinegar, olive oil, salt and pepper.
6. In a salad bowl, combine the rocket with the cooled figs and chickpeas.
7. Toss with the sauce and serve.

Sweet Potatoes with Tofu

Prep time: 15 minutes | Cook time: 35 minutes | Serves 8

8 sweet potatoes, scrubbed
2 tbsps. olive oil
1 large onion, chopped
2 green chilies, deseeded and chopped
227 g tofu, crumbled

2 tbsps. Cajun seasoning
200 g chopped tomatoes
1 can kidney beans, drained and rinsed
Salt and ground black pepper, to taste

1. Preheat the air fryer to 200ºC.
2. With a knife, pierce the skin of the sweet potatoes and air fry in the air fryer for 30 minutes or until soft.
3. Remove from the air fryer, halve each potato, and set to one side.
4. Over a medium heat, fry the onions and chilies in the olive oil in a skillet for 2 minutes until fragrant.
5. Add the tofu and Cajun seasoning and air fry for a further 3 minutes before incorporating the kidney beans and tomatoes. Sprinkle some salt and pepper as desire.
6. Top each sweet potato halve with a spoonful of the tofu mixture and serve.

Rice and Aubergine Bowl

Prep time: 15 minutes | Cook time: 10 minutes | Serves 4

25 g sliced cucumber
1 tsp. salt
1 tbsp. sugar
7 tbsps. Japanese rice vinegar
3 medium aubergines, sliced

3 tbsps. sweet white miso paste
1 tbsp. mirin rice wine
900 g cooked sushi rice
4 spring onions
1 tbsp. toasted sesame seeds

1. Coat the cucumber slices with the rice wine vinegar, salt, and sugar.
2. Put a dish on top of the bowl to weight it down completely.
3. In a bowl, mix the aubergines, mirin rice wine, and miso paste. Allow to marinate for half an hour.
4. Preheat the air fryer to 200ºC.
5. Put the aubergine slices in the air fryer and air fry for 10 minutes.
6. Fill the bottom of a serving bowl with rice and top with the aubergines and pickled cucumbers.
7. Add the spring onions and sesame seeds for garnish. Serve immediately.

Chapter 4 Poultry

Crispy Chicken Strips

Prep time: 15 minutes | Cook time: 20 minutes | Serves 4

1 tbsp. olive oil
454 g boneless, skinless chicken tenderloins
1 tsp. salt
½ tsp. freshly ground black pepper
½ tsp. paprika
½ tsp. garlic powder
60 g whole-wheat seasoned bread crumbs
1 tsp. dried parsley
Cooking spray

1. Preheat the air fryer to 190ºC. Spray the air fryer basket lightly with cooking spray.
2. In a medium bowl, toss the chicken with the salt, pepper, paprika, and garlic powder until evenly coated.
3. Add the olive oil and toss to coat the chicken evenly.
4. In a separate, shallow bowl, mix together the bread crumbs and parsley.
5. Coat each piece of chicken evenly in the bread crumb mixture.
6. Place the chicken in the air fryer basket in a single layer and spray it lightly with cooking spray. You may need to cook them in batches.
7. Air fry for 10 minutes. Flip the chicken over, lightly spray it with cooking spray, and air fry for an additional 8 to 10 minutes, until golden brown. Serve.

Piri-Piri Chicken Thighs

Prep time: 5 minutes | Cook time: 25 minutes | Serves 4

60 g piri-piri sauce
1 tbsp. freshly squeezed lemon juice
2 tbsps. brown sugar, divided
2 cloves garlic, minced
1 tbsp. extra-virgin olive oil
4 bone-in, skin-on chicken thighs, each weighing approximately 198 to 227 g
½ tsp. cornflour

1. To make the marinade, whisk together the piri-piri sauce, lemon juice, 1 tbsp. of brown sugar, and the garlic in a small bowl. While whisking, slowly pour in the oil in a steady stream and continue to whisk until emulsified. Using a skewer, poke holes in the chicken thighs and place them in a small glass dish. Pour the marinade over the chicken and turn the thighs to coat them with the sauce. Cover the dish and refrigerate for at least 15 minutes and up to 1 hour.
2. Preheat the air fryer to 190ºC. Remove the chicken thighs from the dish, reserving the marinade, and place them skin-side down in the air fryer basket. Air fry until the internal temperature reaches 75ºC, 15 to 20 minutes.
3. Meanwhile, whisk the remaining brown sugar and the cornflour into the marinade and microwave it on high power for 1 minute until it is bubbling and thickened to a glaze.
4. Once the chicken is cooked, turn the thighs over and brush them with the glaze. Air fry for a few additional minutes until the glaze browns and begins to char in spots.
5. Remove the chicken to a platter and serve with additional piri-piri sauce, if desired.

Nutty Chicken Tenders

Prep time: 5 minutes | Cook time: 12 minutes | Serves 4

454 g chicken tenders
1 tsp. salt
1 tsp. black pepper
½ tsp. smoked paprika

60 g coarse mustard
2 tbsps. honey
125 g finely crushed pecans

1. Preheat the air fryer to 180ºC.
2. Place the chicken in a large bowl. Sprinkle with the salt, pepper, and paprika. Toss until the chicken is coated with the spices. Add the mustard and honey and toss until the chicken is coated.
3. Place the pecans on a plate. Working with one piece of chicken at a time, roll the chicken in the pecans until both sides are coated. Lightly brush off any loose pecans. Place the chicken in the air fryer basket.
4. Bake for 12 minutes, or until the chicken is cooked through and the pecans are golden brown.
5. Serve warm.

Honey Rosemary Chicken

Prep time: 10 minutes | Cook time: 20 minutes | Serves 4

60 ml balsamic vinegar
85 g honey
2 tbsps. olive oil
1 tbsp. dried rosemary leaves
1 tsp. salt
½ tsp. freshly ground black pepper
2 whole boneless, skinless chicken breasts (454 g each), halved
Cooking spray

1. In a large resealable bag, combine the vinegar, honey, olive oil, rosemary, salt, and pepper. Add the chicken pieces, seal the bag, and refrigerate to marinate for at least 2 hours.
2. Preheat the air fryer to 160ºC. Line the air fryer basket with parchment paper.
3. Remove the chicken from the marinade and place it on the parchment. Spritz with cooking spray.
4. Bake for 10 minutes. Flip the chicken, spritz it with cooking spray, and bake for 10 minutes more until the internal temperature reaches 75ºC and the chicken is no longer pink inside. Let sit for 5 minutes before serving.

Fried Buffalo Chicken Taquitos

Prep time: 15 minutes | Cook time: 5 to 10 minutes | Serves 6

227 g fat-free cream cheese, softened
30 g Buffalo sauce
280 g shredded cooked chicken
14-cm low-carb flour tortillas
Olive oil spray

1. Preheat the air fryer to 180ºC. Spray the air fryer basket lightly with olive oil spray.
2. In a large bowl, mix together the cream cheese and Buffalo sauce until well combined. Add the chicken and stir

until combined.

3. Place the tortillas on a clean workspace. Spoon 2 to 3 tbsps. of the chicken mixture in a thin line down the centre of each tortilla. Roll up the tortillas.
4. Place the tortillas in the air fryer basket, seam-side down. Spray each tortilla lightly with olive oil spray. You may need to cook the taquitos in batches.
5. Air fry until golden brown, 5 to 10 minutes. Serve hot.

Sweet-and-Sour Drumsticks

Prep time: 5 minutes | Cook time: 23 to 25 minutes | Serves 4

6 chicken drumsticks
3 tbsps. lemon juice, divided
3 tbsps. low-sodium soy sauce, divided
1 tbsp. peanut oil
3 tbsps. honey
3 tbsps. brown sugar
2 tbsps. ketchup
60 ml pineapple juice

1. Preheat the air fryer to 180ºC.
2. Sprinkle the drumsticks with 1 tbsp. of lemon juice and 1 tbsp. of soy sauce. Place in the air fryer basket and drizzle with the peanut oil. Toss to coat. Bake for 18 minutes or until the chicken is almost done.
3. Meanwhile, in a metal bowl, combine the remaining 2 tbsps. of lemon juice, the remaining 2 tbsps. of soy sauce, honey, brown sugar, ketchup, and pineapple juice.
4. Add the cooked chicken to the bowl and stir to coat the chicken well with the sauce.
5. Place the metal bowl in the basket. Bake for 5 to 7 minutes or until the chicken is glazed and registers 75ºC on a meat thermometer. Serve warm.

Potato Cheese Crusted Chicken

Prep time: 15 minutes | Cook time: 22 to 25 minutes | Serves 4

60 ml buttermilk
1 large egg, beaten
182 g instant potato flakes
22 g grated Parmesan cheese
1 tsp. salt
½ tsp. freshly ground black pepper
2 whole boneless, skinless chicken breasts (454 g each), halved
Cooking spray

1. Preheat the air fryer to 160ºC. Line the air fryer basket with parchment paper.
2. In a shallow bowl, whisk the buttermilk and egg until blended. In another shallow bowl, stir together the potato flakes, cheese, salt, and pepper.
3. One at a time, dip the chicken pieces in the buttermilk mixture and the potato flake mixture, coating thoroughly.
4. Place the coated chicken on the parchment and spritz with cooking spray.
5. Bake for 15 minutes. Flip the chicken, spritz it with cooking spray, and bake for 7 to 10 minutes more until the outside is crispy and the inside is no longer pink. Serve immediately.

Chicken Satay with Peanut Sauce

Prep time: 12 minutes | Cook time: 12 to 18 minutes | Serves 4

120 g crunchy peanut butter
80 ml chicken stock
3 tbsps. low-sodium soy sauce
2 tbsps. lemon juice

2 cloves garlic, minced
2 tbsps. olive oil
1 tsp. curry powder
454 g chicken tenders

1. Preheat the air fryer to 200ºC.
2. In a medium bowl, combine the peanut butter, chicken stock, soy sauce, lemon juice, garlic, olive oil, and curry powder, and mix well with a wire whisk until smooth. Remove 2 tbsps. of this mixture to a small bowl. Put remaining sauce into a serving bowl and set aside.
3. Add the chicken tenders to the bowl with the 2 tbsps. sauce and stir to coat. Let stand for a few minutes to marinate, then run a bamboo skewer through each chicken tender lengthwise.
4. Put the chicken in the air fryer basket and air fry in batches for 6 to 9 minutes or until the chicken reaches 75ºC on a meat thermometer. Serve the chicken with the reserved sauce.

Crisp Paprika Chicken Drumsticks

Prep time: 5 minutes | Cook time: 22 minutes | Serves 2

2 tsps. paprika
1 tsp. brown sugar
1 tsp. garlic powder
½ tsp. dry mustard
½ tsp. salt

Pinch pepper
4 (142-g) chicken drumsticks, trimmed
1 tsp. vegetable oil
1 spring onion, green part only, sliced thin on bias

1. Preheat the air fryer to 200ºC.
2. Combine paprika, sugar, garlic powder, mustard, salt, and pepper in a bowl. Pat drumsticks dry with paper towels. Using metal skewer, poke 10 to 15 holes in skin of each drumstick. Rub with oil and sprinkle evenly with spice mixture.
3. Arrange drumsticks in air fryer basket, spaced evenly apart, alternating ends. Air fry until chicken is crisp and registers 91ºC, 22 to 25 minutes, flipping chicken halfway through cooking.
4. Transfer chicken to serving platter, tent loosely with aluminum foil, and let rest for 5 minutes. Sprinkle with spring onion and serve.

Roasted Chicken Tenders with Veggies

Prep time: 10 minutes | Cook time: 18 to 20 minutes | Serves 4

454 g chicken tenders
1 tbsp. honey
Pinch salt
Freshly ground black pepper, to taste
60 g soft fresh bread crumbs

½ tsp. dried thyme
1 tbsp. olive oil
2 carrots, sliced
12 small red potatoes

1. Preheat the air fryer to 190ºC.
2. In a medium bowl, toss the chicken tenders with the honey, salt, and pepper.

3. In a shallow bowl, combine the bread crumbs, thyme, and olive oil, and mix.
4. Coat the tenders in the bread crumbs, pressing firmly onto the meat.
5. Place the carrots and potatoes in the air fryer basket and top with the chicken tenders.
6. Roast for 18 to 20 minutes or until the chicken is cooked to 75ºC and the vegetables are tender, shaking the basket halfway during the cooking time.
7. Serve warm.

Dill Chicken Strips

Prep time: 15 minutes | Cook time: 10 minutes | Serves 4

2 whole boneless, skinless chicken breasts, halved lengthwise
240 ml Italian dressing
95 g finely crushed potato chips
1 tbsp. dried dill weed
1 tbsp. garlic powder
1 large egg, beaten
Cooking spray

1. In a large resealable bag, combine the chicken and Italian dressing. Seal the bag and refrigerate to marinate at least 1 hour.
2. In a shallow dish, stir together the potato chips, dill, and garlic powder. Place the beaten egg in a second shallow dish.
3. Remove the chicken from the marinade. Roll the chicken pieces in the egg and the potato chip mixture, coating thoroughly.
4. Preheat the air fryer to 160ºC. Line the air fryer basket with parchment paper.
5. Place the coated chicken on the parchment and spritz with cooking spray.
6. Bake for 5 minutes. Flip the chicken, spritz it with cooking spray, and bake for 5 minutes more until the outsides are crispy and the insides are no longer pink. Serve immediately.

Lemon Parmesan Chicken

Prep time: 10 minutes | Cook time: 20 minutes | Serves 4

1 egg
2 tbsps. lemon juice
2 tsps. minced garlic
½ tsp. salt
½ tsp. freshly ground black pepper
4 boneless, skinless chicken breasts, thin cut
Olive oil spray
60 g whole-wheat bread crumbs
22 g grated Parmesan cheese

1. In a medium bowl, whisk together the egg, lemon juice, garlic, salt, and pepper. Add the chicken breasts, cover, and refrigerate for up to 1 hour.
2. In a shallow bowl, combine the bread crumbs and Parmesan cheese.
3. Preheat the air fryer to 180ºC. Spray the air fryer basket lightly with olive oil spray.
4. Remove the chicken breasts from the egg mixture, then dredge them in the bread crumb mixture, and place in the air fryer basket in a single layer. Lightly spray the chicken breasts with olive oil spray. You may need to cook the chicken in batches.
5. Air fry for 8 minutes. Flip the chicken over, lightly spray with olive oil spray, and air fry until the chicken reaches an internal temperature of 75ºC, for an additional 7 to 12 minutes.
6. Serve warm.

Blackened Chicken Breasts

Prep time: 10 minutes | Cook time: 20 minutes | Serves 4

1 large egg, beaten
150 g Blackened seasoning
2 whole boneless, skinless chicken breasts (454 g

each), halved
Cooking spray

1. Preheat the air fryer to 180ºC. Line the air fryer basket with parchment paper.
2. Place the beaten egg in one shallow bowl and the Blackened seasoning in another shallow bowl.
3. One at a time, dip the chicken pieces in the beaten egg and the Blackened seasoning, coating thoroughly.
4. Place the chicken pieces on the parchment and spritz with cooking spray.
5. Air fry for 10 minutes. Flip the chicken, spritz it with cooking spray, and air fry for 10 minutes more until the internal temperature reaches 75ºC and the chicken is no longer pink inside. Let sit for 5 minutes before serving.

Celery Chicken

Prep time: 10 minutes | Cook time: 15 minutes | Serves 4

120 ml soy sauce
2 tbsps. hoisin sauce
4 tsps. minced garlic
1 tsp. freshly ground black pepper

8 boneless, skinless chicken tenderloins
100 g chopped celery
1 medium red pepper, diced
Olive oil spray

1. Preheat the air fryer to 190ºC. Spray the air fryer basket lightly with olive oil spray.
2. In a large bowl, mix together the soy sauce, hoisin sauce, garlic, and black pepper to make a marinade. Add the chicken, celery, and pepper and toss to coat.
3. Shake the excess marinade off the chicken, place it and the vegetables in the air fryer basket, and lightly spray with olive oil spray. You may need to cook them in batches. Reserve the remaining marinade.
4. Air fry for 8 minutes. Turn the chicken over and brush with some of the remaining marinade. Air fry for an additional 5 to 7 minutes, or until the chicken reaches an internal temperature of at least 75ºC. Serve.

Fajita Chicken Strips

Prep time: 10 minutes | Cook time: 15 minutes | Serves 4

454 g boneless, skinless chicken tenderloins, cut into strips
3 peppers, any colour, cut into chunks
1 onion, cut into chunks

1 tbsp. olive oil
1 tbsp. fajita seasoning mix
Cooking spray

1. Preheat the air fryer to 190ºC.
2. In a large bowl, mix together the chicken, peppers, onion, olive oil, and fajita seasoning mix until completely coated.
3. Spray the air fryer basket lightly with cooking spray.
4. Place the chicken and vegetables in the air fryer basket and lightly spray with cooking spray.
5. Air fry for 7 minutes. Shake the basket and air fry for an additional 5 to 8 minutes, until the chicken is cooked through and the veggies are starting to char.
6. Serve warm.

Chicken-Lettuce Wraps

Prep time: 15 minutes | Cook time: 12 to 16 minutes | Serves 2 to 4

454 g boneless, skinless chicken thighs, trimmed
1 tsp. vegetable oil
2 tbsps. lime juice
1 shallot, minced
1 tbsp. fish sauce, plus extra for serving
2 tsps. packed brown sugar
1 garlic clove, minced
⅛ tsp. red pepper flakes

1 mango, peeled, pitted, and cut into ½–cm pieces
25 g chopped fresh mint
25 g chopped fresh coriander
25 g chopped fresh Thai basil
1 head Bibb lettuce, leaves separated (227 g)
30 g chopped dry-roasted peanuts
2 Thai chilies, stemmed and sliced thin

1. Preheat the air fryer to 205ºC.
2. Pat the chicken dry with paper towels and rub with oil. Place the chicken in air fryer basket and air fry for 12 to 16 minutes, or until the chicken registers 80ºC, flipping and rotating chicken halfway through cooking.
3. Meanwhile, whisk lime juice, shallot, fish sauce, sugar, garlic, and pepper flakes together in large bowl; set aside.
4. Transfer chicken to cutting board, let cool slightly, then shred into bite-size pieces using 2 forks. Add the shredded chicken, mango, mint, coriander, and basil to bowl with dressing and toss to coat.
5. Serve the chicken in the lettuce leaves, passing peanuts, Thai chilies, and extra fish sauce separately.

Israeli Chicken Schnitzel

Prep time: 5 minutes | Cook time: 10 minutes | Serves 4

2 large boneless, skinless chicken breasts, each weighing about 454 g
125 g plain flour
2 tsps. garlic powder
2 tsps. salt
1 tsp. black pepper

1 tsp. paprika
2 eggs beaten with 2 tbsps. water
240 g panko bread crumbs
Vegetable oil spray
Lemon juice, for serving

1. Preheat the air fryer to 190ºC.
2. Place 1 chicken breast between 2 pieces of plastic wrap. Use a mallet or a rolling pin to pound the chicken until it is ½ cm thick. Set aside. Repeat with the second breast. Whisk together the flour, garlic powder, salt, pepper, and paprika on a large plate. Place the panko in a separate shallow bowl or pie plate.
3. Dredge 1 chicken breast in the flour, shaking off any excess, then dip it in the egg mixture. Dredge the chicken breast in the panko, making sure to coat it completely. Shake off any excess panko. Place the battered chicken breast on a plate. Repeat with the second chicken breast.
4. Spray the air fryer basket with oil spray. Place 1 of the battered chicken breasts in the basket and spray the top with oil spray. Air fry until the top is browned, about 5 minutes. Flip the chicken and spray the second side with oil spray. Air fry until the second side is browned and crispy and the internal temperature reaches 75ºC. Remove the first chicken breast from the air fryer and repeat with the second chicken breast.
5. Serve hot with lemon juice.

Air Fryer Naked Chicken Tenders

Prep time: 5 minutes | Cook time: 7 minutes | Serves 4

Seasoning:
1 tsp. salt
½ tsp. garlic powder
½ tsp. onion powder
½ tsp. chili powder

¼ tsp. sweet paprika
¼ tsp. freshly ground black pepper
Chicken:
8 chicken breast tenders (454 g total)
2 tbsps. mayonnaise

1. Preheat the air fryer to 190ºC.
2. For the seasoning: In a small bowl, combine the salt, garlic powder, onion powder, chili powder, paprika, and pepper.
3. For the chicken: Place the chicken in a medium bowl and add the mayonnaise. Mix well to coat all over, then sprinkle with the seasoning mix.
4. Working in batches, arrange a single layer of the chicken in the air fryer basket. Air fry for 6 to 7 minutes, flipping halfway, until cooked through in the centre. Serve immediately.

Chapter 5 Fish and Seafood

Homemade Fish Sticks

Prep time: 15 minutes | Cook time: 10 to 15 minutes | Serves 4

4 fish fillets
66 g whole-wheat flour
1 tsp. seasoned salt
2 eggs
189 g whole-wheat panko bread crumbs
½ tbsp. dried parsley flakes
Cooking spray

1. Preheat the air fryer to 200ºC. Spray the air fryer basket lightly with cooking spray.
2. Cut the fish fillets lengthwise into "sticks."
3. In a shallow bowl, mix the whole-wheat flour and seasoned salt.
4. In a small bowl, whisk the eggs with 1 tsp. of water.
5. In another shallow bowl, mix the panko bread crumbs and parsley flakes.
6. Coat each fish stick in the seasoned flour, then in the egg mixture, and dredge them in the panko bread crumbs.
7. Place the fish sticks in the air fryer basket in a single layer and lightly spray the fish sticks with cooking spray. You may need to cook them in batches.
8. Air fry for 5 to 8 minutes. Flip the fish sticks over and lightly spray with the cooking spray. Air fry until golden brown and crispy, 5 to 7 more minutes.
9. Serve warm.

Marinated Salmon Fillets

Prep time: 10 minutes | Cook time: 15 to 20 minutes | Serves 4

60 ml soy sauce
60 ml rice wine vinegar
1 tbsp. brown sugar
1 tbsp. olive oil
1 tsp. mustard powder
1 tsp. ground ginger
½ tsp. freshly ground black pepper
½ tsp. minced garlic
4 (170-g) salmon fillets, skin-on
Cooking spray

1. In a small bowl, combine the soy sauce, rice wine vinegar, brown sugar, olive oil, mustard powder, ginger, black pepper, and garlic to make a marinade.
2. Place the fillets in a shallow baking dish and pour the marinade over them. Cover the baking dish and marinate for at least 1 hour in the refrigerator, turning the fillets occasionally to keep them coated in the marinade.
3. Preheat the air fryer to 190ºC. Spray the air fryer basket lightly with cooking spray.
4. Shake off as much marinade as possible from the fillets and place them, skin-side down, in the air fryer basket in a single layer. You may need to cook the fillets in batches.
5. Air fry for 15 to 20 minutes for well done. The minimum internal temperature should be 65ºC at the thickest part of the fillets.
6. Serve hot.

Country Prawn

Prep time: 10 minutes | Cook time: 15 to 20 minutes | Serves 4

454 g large prawns, deveined, with tails on
454 g smoked turkey sausage, cut into thick slices
2 corn cobs, quartered
1 courgette, cut into bite-sized pieces

1 red pepper, cut into chunks
1 tbsp. Old Bay seasoning
2 tbsps. olive oil
Cooking spray

1. Preheat the air fryer to 200ºC. Spray the air fryer basket lightly with cooking spray.
2. In a large bowl, mix the prawns, turkey sausage, corn, courgette, pepper, and Old Bay seasoning, and toss to coat with the spices. Add the olive oil and toss again until evenly coated.
3. Spread the mixture in the air fryer basket in a single layer. You will need to cook in batches.
4. Air fry for 15 to 20 minutes, or until cooked through, shaking the basket every 5 minutes for even cooking.
5. Serve immediately.

Cajun-Style Fish Tacos

Prep time: 5 minutes | Cook time: 10 to 15 minutes | Serves 6

2 tsps. avocado oil
1 tbsp. Cajun seasoning
4 tilapia fillets

1 (397-g) package coleslaw mix
12 corn tortillas
2 limes, cut into wedges

1. Preheat the air fryer to 190ºC. Line the air fryer basket with parchment paper.
2. In a medium, shallow bowl, mix the avocado oil and the Cajun seasoning to make a marinade. Add the tilapia fillets and coat evenly.
3. Place the fillets in the basket in a single layer, leaving room between each fillet. You may need to cook in batches.
4. Air fry until the fish is cooked and easily flakes with a fork, 10 to 15 minutes.
5. Assemble the tacos by placing some of the coleslaw mix in each tortilla. Add ⅓ of a tilapia fillet to each tortilla. Squeeze some lime juice over the top of each taco and serve.

Spanish Garlic Prawn

Prep time: 10 minutes | Cook time: 10 to 15 minutes | Serves 4

2 tsps. minced garlic
2 tsps. lemon juice
2 tsps. olive oil
½ to 1 tsp. crushed red pepper
340 g medium prawns, deveined, with tails on
Cooking spray

1. In a medium bowl, mix together the garlic, lemon juice, olive oil, and crushed red pepper to make a marinade.
2. Add the prawns and toss to coat in the marinade. Cover with plastic wrap and place the bowl in the refrigerator for 30 minutes.
3. Preheat the air fryer to 200ºC. Spray the air fryer basket lightly with cooking spray.
4. Place the prawns in the air fryer basket. Air fry for 5 minutes. Shake the basket and air fry until the prawns are cooked through and nicely browned, an additional 5 to 10 minutes. Cool for 5 minutes before serving.

Garlic-Lemon Tilapia

Prep time: 5 minutes | Cook time: 10 to 15 minutes | Serves 4

1 tbsp. lemon juice
1 tbsp. olive oil
1 tsp. minced garlic
½ tsp. chili powder
4 (170-g) tilapia fillets

1. Preheat the air fryer to 190ºC. Line the air fryer basket with parchment paper.
2. In a large, shallow bowl, mix together the lemon juice, olive oil, garlic, and chili powder to make a marinade. Place the tilapia fillets in the bowl and coat evenly.
3. Place the fillets in the basket in a single layer, leaving space between each fillet. You may need to cook in more than one batch.
4. Air fry until the fish is cooked and flakes easily with a fork, 10 to 15 minutes.
5. Serve hot.

Simple Salmon Bites

Prep time: 15 minutes | Cook time: 10 to 15 minutes | Serves 4

4 (142-g) cans pink salmon, skinless, boneless in water, drained
2 eggs, beaten
125 g whole-wheat panko bread crumbs
4 tbsps. finely minced red pepper
2 tbsps. parsley flakes
2 tsps. Old Bay seasoning
Cooking spray

1. Preheat the air fryer to 180ºC.
2. Spray the air fryer basket lightly with cooking spray.
3. In a medium bowl, mix the salmon, eggs, panko bread crumbs, red pepper, parsley flakes, and Old Bay seasoning.
4. Using a small cookie scoop, form the mixture into 20 balls.
5. Place the salmon bites in the air fryer basket in a single layer and spray lightly with cooking spray. You may need to cook them in batches.
6. Air fry until crispy for 10 to 15 minutes, shaking the basket a couple of times for even cooking.
7. Serve immediately.

Crispy Cod Cakes with Salad Greens

Prep time: 15 minutes | Cook time: 12 minutes | Serves 4

454 g cod fillets, cut into chunks
30 g packed fresh basil leaves
3 cloves garlic, crushed
½ tsp. smoked paprika
¼ tsp. salt
¼ tsp. pepper
1 large egg, beaten
125 g panko bread crumbs
Cooking spray

Salad greens, for serving

1. In a food processor, pulse cod, basil, garlic, smoked paprika, salt, and pepper until cod is finely chopped, stirring occasionally. Form into 8 patties, about 4-cm in diameter. Dip each first into the egg, then into the panko, patting to adhere. Spray with oil on one side.
2. Preheat the air fryer to 200ºC.
3. Working in batches, place half the cakes in the basket, oil-side down; spray with oil. Air fry for 12 minutes, until golden brown and cooked through.
4. Serve cod cakes with salad greens.

Tuna Sliders

Prep time: 15 minutes | Cook time: 10 to 15 minutes | Serves 4

3 (142-g) cans tuna, packed in water
85 g whole-wheat panko bread crumbs
30 g shredded Parmesan cheese
1 tbsp. sriracha

¾ tsp. black pepper
10 whole-wheat slider buns
Cooking spray

1. Preheat the air fryer to 180ºC.
2. Spray the air fryer basket lightly with cooking spray.
3. In a medium bowl combine the tuna, bread crumbs, Parmesan cheese, sriracha, and black pepper and stir to combine.
4. Form the mixture into 10 patties.
5. Place the patties in the air fryer basket in a single layer. Spray the patties lightly with cooking spray. You may need to cook them in batches.
6. Air fry for 6 to 8 minutes. Turn the patties over and lightly spray with cooking spray. Air fry until golden brown and crisp, another 4 to 7 more minutes. Serve warm.

Blackened Prawn Tacos

Prep time: 10 minutes | Cook time: 10 to 15 minutes | Serves 4

340 g medium prawns, deveined, with tails off
1 tsp. olive oil
1 to 2 tsps. Blackened seasoning
8 corn tortillas, warmed
1 (397-g) bag coleslaw mix
2 limes, cut in half
Cooking spray

1. Preheat the air fryer to 200ºC.
2. Spray the air fryer basket lightly with cooking spray.
3. Dry the prawns with a paper towel to remove excess water.
4. In a medium bowl, toss the prawns with olive oil and Blackened seasoning.
5. Place the prawns in the air fryer basket and air fry for 5 minutes. Shake the basket, lightly spray with cooking spray, and cook until the prawns are cooked through and starting to brown, 5 to 10 more minutes.
6. Fill each tortilla with the coleslaw mix and top with the blackened prawns. Squeeze fresh lime juice over top and serve.

Spicy Orange Prawn

Prep time: 20 minutes | Cook time: 10 to 15 minutes | Serves 4

80 ml orange juice
3 tsps. minced garlic
1 tsp. Old Bay seasoning
¼ to ½ tsp. cayenne pepper

454 g medium prawns, peeled and deveined, with tails off
Cooking spray

1. In a medium bowl, combine the orange juice, garlic, Old Bay seasoning, and cayenne pepper.
2. Dry the prawns with paper towels to remove excess water.
3. Add the prawns to the marinade and stir to evenly coat. Cover with plastic wrap and place in the refrigerator for 30 minutes so the prawns can soak up the marinade.
4. Preheat the air fryer to 200ºC. Spray the air fryer basket lightly with cooking spray.
5. Place the prawns into the air fryer basket. Air fry for 5 minutes. Shake the basket and lightly spray with olive oil. Air fry until the prawns are opaque and crisp, 5 to 10 more minutes.
6. Serve immediately.

Vegetable and Fish Tacos

Prep time: 10 minutes | Cook time: 9 to 12 minutes | Serves 4

454 g white fish fillets
2 tsps. olive oil
3 tbsps. freshly squeezed lemon juice, divided
30 g chopped red cabbage

1 large carrot, grated
125 g low-sodium salsa
90 g low-fat Greek yogurt
4 soft low-sodium whole-wheat tortillas

1. Preheat the air fryer to 200ºC.
2. Brush the fish with the olive oil and sprinkle with 1 tbsp. of lemon juice. Air fry in the air fryer basket for 9 to 12 minutes, or until the fish just flakes when tested with a fork.
3. Meanwhile, in a medium bowl, stir together the remaining 2 tbsps. of lemon juice, the red cabbage, carrot, salsa, and yogurt.
4. When the fish is cooked, remove it from the air fryer basket and break it up into large pieces.
5. Offer the fish, tortillas, and the cabbage mixture, and let each person assemble a taco.
6. Serve immediately.

Cajun-Style Salmon Burgers

Prep time: 10 minutes | Cook time: 10 to 15 minutes | Serves 4

4 (142-g) cans pink salmon in water, any skin and bones removed, drained
2 eggs, beaten
125 g whole-wheat bread crumbs
4 tbsps. light mayonnaise

2 tsps. Cajun seasoning
2 tsps. dry mustard
4 whole-wheat buns
Cooking spray

1. In a medium bowl, mix the salmon, egg, bread crumbs, mayonnaise, Cajun seasoning, and dry mustard. Cover with plastic wrap and refrigerate for 30 minutes.
2. Preheat the air fryer to 180ºC. Spray the air fryer basket lightly with cooking spray.

3. Shape the mixture into four 1-cm-thick patties about the same size as the buns.
4. Place the salmon patties in the air fryer basket in a single layer and lightly spray the tops with cooking spray. You may need to cook them in batches.
5. Air fry for 6 to 8 minutes. Turn the patties over and lightly spray with cooking spray. Air fry until crispy on the outside, 4 to 7 more minutes.
6. Serve on whole-wheat buns.

Lime-Chili Prawn Bowl

Prep time: 10 minutes | Cook time: 10 to 15 minutes | Serves 4

2 tsps. lime juice
1 tsp. olive oil
1 tsp. honey
1 tsp. minced garlic
1 tsp. chili powder
Salt, to taste

340 g medium prawns, peeled and deveined
530 g cooked brown rice
1 (425-g) can seasoned black beans, warmed
1 large avocado, chopped
210 g sliced cherry tomatoes
Cooking spray

1. Preheat the air fryer to 200ºC. Spray the air fryer basket lightly with cooking spray.
2. In a medium bowl, mix together the lime juice, olive oil, honey, garlic, chili powder, and salt to make a marinade.
3. Add the prawns and toss to coat evenly in the marinade.
4. Place the prawns in the air fryer basket. Air fry for 5 minutes. Shake the basket and air fry until the prawns are cooked through and starting to brown, an additional 5 to 10 minutes.
5. To assemble the bowls, spoon ¼ of the rice, black beans, avocado, and cherry tomatoes into each of four bowls. Top with the prawns and serve.

Sesame Glazed Salmon

Prep time: 5 minutes | Cook time: 12 to 16 minutes | Serves 4

3 tbsps. soy sauce
1 tbsp. rice wine or dry sherry
1 tbsp. brown sugar
1 tbsp. toasted sesame oil
1 tsp. minced garlic

¼ tsp. minced ginger
4 (170-g) salmon fillets, skin-on
½ tbsp. sesame seeds
Cooking spray

1. In a small bowl, mix the soy sauce, rice wine, brown sugar, toasted sesame oil, garlic, and ginger.
2. Place the salmon in a shallow baking dish and pour the marinade over the fillets. Cover and refrigerate for at least 1 hour, turning the fillets occasionally to coat in the marinade.
3. Preheat the air fryer to 190ºC. Spray the air fryer basket lightly with cooking spray.
4. Shake off as much marinade as possible and place the fillets, skin-side down, in the air fryer basket in a single layer. Reserve the marinade. You may need to cook them in batches.
5. Air fry for 8 to 10 minutes. Brush the tops of the salmon fillets with the reserved marinade and sprinkle with sesame seeds.
6. Increase the temperature to 200ºC and air fry for 2 to 5 more minutes for medium, 1 to 3 minutes for medium rare, or 4 to 6 minutes for well done.
7. Serve warm.

Seasoned Breaded Prawn

Prep time: 15 minutes | Cook time: 10 to 15 minutes | Serves 4

2 tsps. Old Bay seasoning, divided
½ tsp. garlic powder
½ tsp. onion powder
454 g large prawns, deveined, with tails on

2 large eggs
62 g whole-wheat panko bread crumbs
Cooking spray

1. Preheat the air fryer to 190ºC.
2. Spray the air fryer basket lightly with cooking spray.
3. In a medium bowl, mix together 1 tsp. of Old Bay seasoning, garlic powder, and onion powder. Add the prawns and toss with the seasoning mix to lightly coat.
4. In a separate small bowl, whisk the eggs with 1 tsp. water.
5. In a shallow bowl, mix together the remaining 1 tsp. Old Bay seasoning and the panko bread crumbs.
6. Dip each prawns in the egg mixture and dredge in the bread crumb mixture to evenly coat.
7. Place the prawns in the air fryer basket, in a single layer. Lightly spray the prawns with cooking spray. You many need to cook the prawns in batches.
8. Air fry for 10 to 15 minutes, or until the prawns is cooked through and crispy, shaking the basket at 5-minute intervals to redistribute and evenly cook.
9. Serve immediately.

Air Fried Spring Rolls

Prep time: 10 minutes | Cook time: 17 to 22 minutes | Serves 4

2 tsps. minced garlic
40 g finely sliced cabbage
135 g matchstick cut carrots
2 (113-g) cans tiny prawns, drained

4 tsps. soy sauce
Salt and freshly ground black pepper, to taste
16 square spring roll wrappers
Cooking spray

1. Preheat the air fryer to 190ºC.
2. Spray the air fryer basket lightly with cooking spray. Spray a medium sauté pan with cooking spray.
3. Add the garlic to the sauté pan and cook over medium heat until fragrant, 30 to 45 seconds. Add the cabbage and carrots and sauté until the vegetables are slightly tender, about 5 minutes.
4. Add the prawns and soy sauce and season with salt and pepper, then stir to combine. Sauté until the moisture has evaporated, 2 more minutes. Set aside to cool.
5. Place a spring roll wrapper on a work surface so it looks like a diamond. Place 1 tbsp. of the prawn mixture on the lower end of the wrapper.
6. Roll the wrapper away from you halfway, then fold in the right and left sides, like an envelope. Continue to roll to the very end, using a little water to seal the edge. Repeat with the remaining wrappers and filling.
7. Place the spring rolls in the air fryer basket in a single layer, leaving room between each roll. Lightly spray with cooking spray. You may need to cook them in batches.
8. Air fry for 5 minutes. Turn the rolls over, lightly spray with cooking spray, and air fry until heated through and the rolls start to brown, 5 to 10 more minutes. Cool for 5 minutes before serving.

Chapter 6 Beef, Lamb and Pork

Avocado Buttered Flank Steak

Prep time: 5 minutes | Cook time: 12 minutes | Serves 1

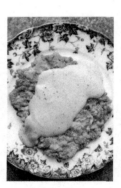

1 flank steak
Salt and ground black pepper, to taste
2 avocados
2 tbsps. butter, melted
120 ml chimichurri sauce

1. Rub the flank steak with salt and pepper to taste and leave to sit for 20 minutes.
2. Preheat the air fryer to 200ºC and place a rack inside.
3. Halve the avocados and take out the pits. Spoon the flesh into a bowl and mash with a fork. Mix in the melted butter and chimichurri sauce, making sure everything is well combined.
4. Put the steak in the air fryer and air fry for 6 minutes. Flip over and allow to air fry for another 6 minutes.
5. Serve the steak with the avocado butter.

Chicken Fried Steak

Prep time: 15 minutes | Cook time: 10 minutes | Serves 4

62 g flour
2 tsps. salt, divided
Freshly ground black pepper, to taste
¼ tsp. garlic powder
240 ml buttermilk
120 g fine bread crumbs
4 (170-g) tenderized top round steaks, 1-cm thick
Vegetable or rapeseed oil
For the Gravy:
2 tbsps. butter or bacon drippings
¼ onion, minced
1 clove garlic, smashed
¼ tsp. dried thyme
3 tbsps. flour
240 ml milk
Salt and freshly ground black pepper, to taste
Dashes of Worcestershire sauce

1. Set up a dredging station. Combine the flour, 1 tsp. of salt, black pepper and garlic powder in a shallow bowl. Pour the buttermilk into a second shallow bowl. Finally, put the bread crumbs and 1 tsp. of salt in a third shallow bowl.
2. Dip the tenderized steaks into the flour, then the buttermilk, and then the bread crumb mixture, pressing the crumbs onto the steak. Put them on a baking sheet and spray both sides generously with vegetable or rapeseed oil.
3. Preheat the air fryer to 200ºC.
4. Transfer the steaks to the air fryer basket, two at a time, and air fry for 10 minutes, flipping the steaks over halfway through the cooking time. Hold the first batch of steaks warm in a 80ºC oven while you air fry the second batch.
5. While the steaks are cooking, make the gravy. Melt the butter in a small saucepan over medium heat on the

stovetop. Add the onion, garlic and thyme and cook for five minutes, until the onion is soft and just starting to brown. Stir in the flour and cook for another five minutes, stirring regularly, until the mixture starts to brown. Whisk in the milk and bring the mixture to a boil to thicken. Season to taste with salt, lots of freshly ground black pepper, and a few dashes of Worcestershire sauce.

6. Pour the gravy over the chicken fried steaks and serve.

Air Fried Ribeye Steak

Prep time: 5 minutes | Cook time: 15 minutes | Serves 1

1 (454-g) ribeye steak
Salt and ground black pepper, to taste
1 tbsp. peanut oil
½ tbsp. butter
½ tsp. thyme, chopped

1. Preheat a skillet in the air fryer at 200ºC.
2. Season the steaks with salt and pepper. Remove the skillet from the air fryer once preheated.
3. Put the skillet on the stovetop burner on a medium heat and drizzle with the peanut oil.
4. Sear the steak for 2 minutes.
5. Turn over the steak and place in the air fryer for 6 minutes.
6. Take out the steak from the air fryer and place it back on the stove top on low heat to keep warm.
7. Toss in the butter and thyme and air fry for 3 minutes.
8. Rest for 5 minutes and serve.

Marinated Pork Tenderloin

Prep time: 10 minutes | Cook time: 30 minutes | Serves 4 to 6

60 ml olive oil
60 ml soy sauce
60 ml freshly squeezed lemon juice
1 garlic clove, minced
1 tbsp. Dijon mustard
1 tsp. salt
½ tsp. freshly ground black pepper
907 g pork tenderloin

1. In a large mixing bowl, make the marinade: Mix the olive oil, soy sauce, lemon juice, minced garlic, Dijon mustard, salt, and pepper. Reserve ¼ cup of the marinade.
2. Put the tenderloin in a large bowl and pour the remaining marinade over the meat. Cover and marinate in the refrigerator for about 1 hour.
3. Preheat the air fryer to 200ºC.
4. Put the marinated pork tenderloin into the air fryer basket. Roast for 10 minutes. Flip the pork and baste it with half of the reserved marinade. Roast for 10 minutes more.
5. Flip the pork, then baste with the remaining marinade. Roast for another 10 minutes, for a total cooking time of 30 minutes.
6. Serve immediately.

Herbed Beef

Prep time: 5 minutes | Cook time: 22 minutes | Serves 6

1 tsp. dried dill
1 tsp. dried thyme
1 tsp. garlic powder
907 g beef steak
3 tbsps. butter

1. Preheat the air fryer to 180ºC.
2. Combine the dill, thyme, and garlic powder in a small bowl, and massage into the steak.
3. Air fry the steak in the air fryer for 20 minutes, then remove, shred, and return to the air fryer.
4. Add the butter and air fry the shredded steak for a further 2 minutes at 185ºC. Make sure the beef is coated in the butter before serving.

Greek Lamb Rack

Prep time: 5 minutes | Cook time: 10 minutes | Serves 4

60 ml freshly squeezed lemon juice
1 tsp. oregano
2 tsps. minced fresh rosemary
1 tsp. minced fresh thyme
2 tbsps. minced garlic
Salt and freshly ground black pepper, to taste
2 to 4 tbsps. olive oil
1 lamb rib rack (7 to 8 ribs)

1. Preheat the air fryer to 180ºC.
2. In a small mixing bowl, combine the lemon juice, oregano, rosemary, thyme, garlic, salt, pepper, and olive oil and mix well.
3. Rub the mixture over the lamb, covering all the meat. Put the rack of lamb in the air fryer. Roast for 10 minutes. Flip the rack halfway through.
4. After 10 minutes, measure the internal temperature of the rack of lamb reaches at least 65ºC.
5. Serve immediately.

Kielbasa Sausage with Pierogies

Prep time: 15 minutes | Cook time: 30 minutes | Serves 3 to 4

1 sweet onion, sliced
1 tsp. olive oil
Salt and freshly ground black pepper, to taste
2 tbsps. butter, cut into small cubes
1 tsp. sugar

454 g light Polish kielbasa sausage, cut into 4-cm chunks
1 (369-g) package frozen mini pierogies
2 tsps. vegetable or olive oil
Chopped spring onions, for garnish

1. Preheat the air fryer to 200ºC.
2. Toss the sliced onions with olive oil, salt and pepper and transfer them to the air fryer basket. Dot the onions

with pieces of butter and air fry for 2 minutes. Then sprinkle the sugar over the onions and stir. Pour any melted butter from the bottom of the air fryer drawer over the onions. Continue to air fry for another 13 minutes, stirring or shaking the basket every few minutes to air fry the onions evenly.

3. Add the kielbasa chunks to the onions and toss. Air fry for another 5 minutes, shaking the basket halfway through the cooking time. Transfer the kielbasa and onions to a bowl and cover with aluminum foil to keep warm.

4. Toss the frozen pierogies with the vegetable or olive oil and transfer them to the air fryer basket. Air fry at 200ºC for 8 minutes, shaking the basket twice during the cooking time.

5. When the pierogies have finished cooking, return the kielbasa and onions to the air fryer and gently toss with the pierogies. Air fry for 2 more minutes and then transfer everything to a serving platter. Garnish with the chopped spring onions and serve hot with the spicy sour cream sauce below.

Beef Stuffed Peppers

Prep time: 10 minutes | Cook time: 30 minutes | Serves 4

454 g beef mince
1 tbsp. taco seasoning mix
1 can diced tomatoes and green chilies

4 green peppers
90 g shredded Monterey jack cheese, divided

1. Preheat the air fryer to 180ºC.
2. Set a skillet over a high heat and cook the beef mince for 8 minutes. Make sure it is cooked through and browned all over. Drain the fat.
3. Stir in the taco seasoning mix, and the diced tomatoes and green chilies. Allow the mixture to cook for a further 4 minutes.
4. In the meantime, slice the tops off the green peppers and remove the seeds and membranes.
5. When the meat mixture is fully cooked, spoon equal amounts of it into the peppers and top with the Monterey jack cheese. Then place the peppers into the air fryer. Air fry for 15 minutes.
6. The peppers are ready when they are soft, and the cheese is bubbling and brown. Serve warm.

Crumbed Golden Filet Mignon

Prep time: 15 minutes | Cook time: 12 minutes | Serves 4

227 g filet mignon
Sea salt and ground black pepper, to taste
½ tsp. cayenne pepper
1 tsp. dried basil
1 tsp. dried rosemary

1 tsp. dried thyme
1 tbsp. sesame oil
1 small egg, whisked
60 g bread crumbs

1. Preheat the air fryer to 180ºC.
2. Cover the filet mignon with the salt, black pepper, cayenne pepper, basil, rosemary, and thyme. Coat with sesame oil.
3. Put the egg in a shallow plate.
4. Pour the bread crumbs in another plate.
5. Dip the filet mignon into the egg. Roll it into the crumbs.
6. Transfer the steak to the air fryer and air fry for 12 minutes or until it turns golden.
7. Serve immediately.

Beef Chuck Cheeseburgers

Prep time: 10 minutes | Cook time: 15 minutes | Serves 4

340 g chuck beef mince
1 envelope onion soup mix
Salt and freshly ground black pepper, to taste

1 tsp. paprika
4 slices Monterey Jack cheese
4 ciabatta rolls

1. In a bowl, stir together the ground chuck, onion soup mix, salt, black pepper, and paprika to combine well.
2. Preheat the air fryer to 195ºC.
3. Take four equal portions of the mixture and mold each one into a patty. Transfer to the air fryer and air fry for 10 minutes.
4. Put the slices of cheese on the top of the burgers.
5. Air fry for another minute before serving on ciabatta rolls.

Pork Medallions with Radicchio and Endive Salad

Prep time: 25 minutes | Cook time: 7 minutes | Serves 4

1 (227-g) pork tenderloin
Salt and freshly ground black pepper, to taste
30 g flour
2 eggs, lightly beaten
80 g crushed crackers
1 tsp. paprika
1 tsp. dry mustard
1 tsp. garlic powder
1 tsp. dried thyme
1 tsp. salt
vegetable or rapeseed oil, in spray bottle
Vinaigrette:
60 ml white balsamic vinegar

2 tbsps. agave syrup (or honey or maple syrup)
1 tbsp. Dijon mustard
juice of ½ lemon
2 tbsps. chopped chervil or flat-leaf parsley
salt and freshly ground black pepper
120 ml extra-virgin olive oil
Radicchio and Endive Salad:
1 heart romaine lettuce, torn into large pieces
½ head radicchio, coarsely chopped
2 heads endive, sliced
100 g cherry tomatoes, halved
85 g fresh Mozzarella, diced
Salt and freshly ground black pepper, to taste

1. Slice the pork tenderloin into 2-cm slices. Using a meat pounder, pound the pork slices into thin 1-cm medallions. Generously season the pork with salt and freshly ground black pepper on both sides.
2. Set up a dredging station using three shallow dishes. Put the flour in one dish and the beaten eggs in a second dish. Combine the cracker meal, paprika, dry mustard, garlic powder, thyme and salt in a third dish.
3. Preheat the air fryer to 200ºC.
4. Dredge the pork medallions in flour first and then into the beaten egg. Let the excess egg drip off and coat both sides of the medallions with the cracker meal crumb mixture. Spray both sides of the coated medallions with vegetable or rapeseed oil.
5. Air fry the medallions in two batches at 200ºC for 5 minutes. Once you have air-fried all the medallions, flip them all over and return the first batch of medallions back into the air fryer on top of the second batch. Air fry at 200ºC for an additional 2 minutes.
6. While the medallions are cooking, make the salad and dressing. Whisk the white balsamic vinegar, agave syrup, Dijon mustard, lemon juice, chervil, salt and pepper together in a small bowl. Whisk in the olive oil slowly until combined and thickened.
7. Combine the romaine lettuce, radicchio, endive, cherry tomatoes, and Mozzarella cheese in a large salad bowl. Drizzle the dressing over the vegetables and toss to combine. Season with salt and freshly ground black pepper.
8. Serve the pork medallions warm on or beside the salad.

Beef Loin with Thyme and Parsley

Prep time: 5 minutes | Cook time: 15 minutes | Serves 4

1 tbsp. butter, melted
¼ dried thyme
1 tsp. garlic salt

¼ tsp. dried parsley
454 g beef loin

1. In a bowl, combine the melted butter, thyme, garlic salt, and parsley.
2. Cut the beef loin into slices and generously apply the seasoned butter using a brush.
3. Preheat the air fryer to 200ºC and place a rack inside.
4. Air fry the beef on the rack for 15 minutes.
5. Take care when removing it and serve hot.

Italian Lamb Chops with Avocado Mayo

Prep time: 5 minutes | Cook time: 12 minutes | Serves 2

2 lamp chops
2 tsps. Italian herbs
2 avocados

115 g mayonnaise
1 tbsp. lemon juice

1. Season the lamb chops with the Italian herbs, then set aside for 5 minutes.
2. Preheat the air fryer to 200ºC and place the rack inside.
3. Put the chops on the rack and air fry for 12 minutes.
4. In the meantime, halve the avocados and open to remove the pits. Spoon the flesh into a blender.
5. Add the mayonnaise and lemon juice and pulse until a smooth consistency is achieved.
6. Take care when removing the chops from the air fryer, then plate up and serve with the avocado mayo.

Cheese Crusted Chops

Prep time: 10 minutes | Cook time: 12 minutes | Serves 4 to 6

¼ tsp. pepper
½ tsp. salt
4 to 6 thick boneless pork chops
110 g pork rind crumbs
¼ tsp. chili powder

½ tsp. onion powder
1 tsp. smoked paprika
2 beaten eggs
3 tbsps. grated Parmesan cheese
Cooking spray

1. Preheat the air fryer to 200ºC.
2. Rub the pepper and salt on both sides of pork chops.
3. In a food processor, pulse pork rinds into crumbs. Mix crumbs with chili powder, onion powder, and paprika in a bowl.
4. Beat eggs in another bowl.
5. Dip pork chops into eggs then into pork rind crumb mixture.
6. Spritz the air fryer with cooking spray and add pork chops to the basket.
7. Air fry for 12 minutes.
8. Serve garnished with the Parmesan cheese.

Greek Lamb Pita Pockets

Prep time: 15 minutes | Cook time: 6 minutes | Serves 4

Dressing:
245 g plain yogurt
1 tbsp. lemon juice
1 tsp. dried dill weed, crushed
1 tsp. ground oregano
½ tsp. salt
Meatballs:
227 g lamb mince
1 tbsp. diced onion
1 tsp. dried parsley
1 tsp. dried dill weed, crushed

¼ tsp. oregano
¼ tsp. coriander
¼ tsp. ground cumin
¼ tsp. salt
4 pita halves
Suggested Toppings:
1 red onion, slivered
1 medium cucumber, deseeded, thinly sliced
Crumbled Feta cheese
Sliced black olives
Chopped fresh peppers

1. Preheat the air fryer to 200ºC.
2. Stir the dressing ingredients together in a small bowl and refrigerate while preparing lamb.
3. Combine all meatball ingredients in a large bowl and stir to distribute seasonings.
4. Shape meat mixture into 12 small meatballs, rounded or slightly flattened if you prefer.
5. Transfer the meatballs in the preheated air fryer and air fry for 6 minutes, until well done. Remove and drain on paper towels.
6. To serve, pile meatballs and the choice of toppings in pita pockets and drizzle with dressing.

Pork Chop Stir Fry

Prep time: 10 minutes | Cook time: 20 minutes | Serves 4

1 tbsp. olive oil
¼ tsp. ground black pepper
½ tsp. salt
1 egg white
4 (113-g) pork chops
72 g almond flour

2 sliced jalapeño peppers
2 sliced spring onions
2 tbsps. olive oil
¼ tsp. ground white pepper
1 tsp. sea salt

1. Coat the air fryer basket with olive oil.
2. Whisk black pepper, salt, and egg white together until foamy.
3. Cut pork chops into pieces, leaving just a bit on bones. Pat dry.
4. Add pieces of pork to egg white mixture, coating well. Let sit for marinade 20 minutes.
5. Preheat the air fryer to 180ºC.
6. Put marinated chops into a large bowl and add almond flour. Dredge and shake off excess and place into air fryer.
7. Air fry the chops in the preheated air fryer for 12 minutes.
8. Turn up the heat to 200ºC and air fry for another 6 minutes until pork chops are nice and crisp.
9. Meanwhile, remove jalapeño seeds and chop up. Chop spring onions and mix with jalapeño pieces.
10. Heat a skillet with olive oil. Stir-fry the white pepper, salt, spring onions, and jalapeños 60 seconds. Then add fried pork pieces to skillet and toss with spring onion mixture. Stir-fry for 1 to 2 minutes until well coated and hot.
11. Serve immediately.

Air Fried Beef Ribs

Prep time: 20 minutes | Cook time: 8 minutes | Serves 4

454 g meaty beef ribs, rinsed and drained
3 tbsps. apple cider vinegar
40 g coriander, finely chopped
1 tbsp. fresh basil leaves, chopped
2 garlic cloves, finely chopped

1 chipotle powder
1 tsp. fennel seeds
1 tsp. hot paprika
Salt and black pepper, to taste
120 ml vegetable oil

1. Coat the ribs with the remaining ingredients and refrigerate for at least 3 hours.
2. Preheat the air fryer to 180ºC.
3. Separate the ribs from the marinade and put them on a grill pan. Air fry for 8 minutes.
4. Pour the remaining marinade over the ribs before serving.

Chapter 7 Starters and Snacks

Cheesy Macaroni Balls

Prep time: 10 minutes | Cook time: 10 minutes | Serves 2

400 g leftover macaroni
90 g shredded Cheddar cheese
65 g flour
120 g bread crumbs
3 large eggs
240 ml milk
½ tsp. salt
¼ tsp. black pepper

1. Preheat the air fryer to 185ºC.
2. In a bowl, combine the leftover macaroni and shredded cheese.
3. Pour the flour in a separate bowl. Put the bread crumbs in a third bowl. Finally, in a fourth bowl, mix the eggs and milk with a whisk.
4. With an ice-cream scoop, create balls from the macaroni mixture. Coat them the flour, then in the egg mixture, and lastly in the bread crumbs.
5. Arrange the balls in the preheated air fryer and air fry for about 10 minutes, giving them an occasional stir. Ensure they crisp up nicely.
6. Serve hot.

Mini Quiche Cups

Prep time: 15 minutes | Cook time: 16 minutes | Makes 10 quiche cups

113 g pork sausage meat
3 eggs
180 ml milk
Cooking spray

113 g sharp Cheddar cheese, grated
Special Equipment:
20 foil muffin cups

1. Preheat the air fryer to 200ºC. Spritz the air fryer basket with cooking spray.
2. Divide sausage into 3 portions and shape each into a thin patty.
3. Put patties in air fryer basket and air fry for 6 minutes.
4. While sausage is cooking, prepare the egg mixture. Combine the eggs and milk in a large bowl and whisk until well blended. Set aside.
5. When sausage has cooked fully, remove patties from the basket, drain well, and use a fork to crumble the meat into small pieces.
6. Double the foil cups into 10 sets. Remove paper liners from the top muffin cups and spray the foil cups lightly with cooking spray.
7. Divide crumbled sausage among the 10 muffin cup sets.
8. Top each with grated cheese, divided evenly among the cups.
9. Put 5 cups in air fryer basket.
10. Pour egg mixture into each cup, filling until each cup is at least ⅔ full.
11. Bake for 8 minutes and test for doneness. A knife inserted into the centre shouldn't have any raw egg on it when removed.
12. Repeat steps 8 through 11 for the remaining quiches.
13. Serve warm.

Pigs in a Blanket

Prep time: 5 minutes | Cook time: 14 minutes | Serves 4 to 6

24 cocktail smoked sausages
6 slices deli-sliced Cheddar cheese, each cut into 8 rectangular pieces
1 (227-g) tube refrigerated crescent roll dough

1. Preheat the air fryer to 180ºC.
2. Unroll the crescent roll dough into one large sheet. If your crescent roll dough has perforated seams, pinch or roll all the perforated seams together. Cut the large sheet of dough into 4 rectangles. Then cut each rectangle into 6 pieces by making one slice lengthwise in the middle and 2 slices horizontally. You should have 24 pieces of dough.
3. Make a deep slit lengthwise down the centre of the cocktail sausage. Stuff two pieces of cheese into the slit in the sausage. Roll one piece of crescent dough around the stuffed cocktail sausage, leaving the ends of the sausage exposed. Pinch the seam together. Repeat with the remaining sausages.
4. Air fry in 2 batches for 7 minutes, placing the sausages seam-side down in the basket. Serve hot.

Crispy Mozzarella Sticks

Prep time: 5 minutes | Cook time: 6 to 7 minutes | Serves 4 to 8

1 egg
1 tbsp. water
8 eggroll wraps
8 Mozzarella string cheese "sticks"

1. Preheat the air fryer to 200ºC.
2. Beat together egg and water in a small bowl.
3. Lay out eggroll wraps and moisten edges with egg wash.
4. Place one piece of string cheese on each wrap near one end.
5. Fold in sides of eggroll wrap over ends of cheese, and then roll up.
6. Brush outside of wrap with egg wash and press gently to seal well.
7. Place in air fryer basket in a single layer and air fry for 5 minutes. Air fry for an additional 1 or 2 minutes, if necessary, or until they are golden brown and crispy.
8. Serve immediately.

Honey Sriracha Chicken Wings

Prep time: 5 minutes | Cook time: 30 minutes | Serves 4

1 tbsp. Sriracha hot sauce
1 tbsp. honey
1 garlic clove, minced
½ tsp. salt
16 chicken wings and drumsticks
Cooking spray

1. Preheat the air fryer to 180ºC.
2. In a large bowl, whisk together the Sriracha hot sauce, honey, minced garlic, and salt, then add the chicken and

toss to coat.

3. Spray the air fryer basket with cooking spray, then place 8 wings in the basket and air fry for 15 minutes, turning halfway through. Repeat this process with the remaining wings.
4. Remove the wings and allow to cool on a wire rack for 10 minutes before serving.

Air Fried Olives

Prep time: 5 minutes | Cook time: 8 minutes | Serves 4

1 (156-g) jar pitted green olives
62 g plain flour
Salt and pepper, to taste
60 g bread crumbs
1 egg
Cooking spray

1. Preheat the air fryer to 200ºC.
2. Remove the olives from the jar and dry thoroughly with paper towels.
3. In a small bowl, combine the flour with salt and pepper to taste. Place the bread crumbs in another small bowl. In a third small bowl, beat the egg.
4. Spritz the air fryer basket with cooking spray.
5. Dip the olives in the flour, then the egg, and then the bread crumbs.
6. Place the breaded olives in the air fryer. It is okay to stack them. Spray the olives with cooking spray. Air fry for 6 minutes. Flip the olives and air fry for an additional 2 minutes, or until brown and crisp.
7. Cool before serving.

Herbed Pita Chips

Prep time: 5 minutes | Cook time: 5 to 6 minutes | Serves 4

¼ tsp. dried basil
¼ tsp. marjoram
¼ tsp. ground oregano
¼ tsp. garlic powder
¼ tsp. ground thyme
¼ tsp. salt
2 whole 12-cm pitas, whole grain or white
Cooking spray

1. Preheat the air fryer to 165ºC.
2. Mix all the seasonings together.
3. Cut each pita half into 4 wedges. Break apart wedges at the fold.
4. Mist one side of pita wedges with oil. Sprinkle with half of seasoning mix.
5. Turn pita wedges over, mist the other side with oil, and sprinkle with remaining seasonings.
6. Place pita wedges in air fryer basket and bake for 2 minutes.
7. Shake the basket and bake for 2 minutes longer. Shake again, and if needed, bake for 1 or 2 more minutes, or until crisp. Watch carefully because at this point they will cook very quickly.
8. Serve hot.

Spicy Chicken Bites

Prep time: 10 minutes | Cook time: 10 to 12 minutes | Makes 30 bites

200 g boneless and skinless chicken thighs, cut into 30 pieces
¼ tsp. salt

2 tbsps. hot sauce
Cooking spray

1. Preheat the air fryer to 200ºC.
2. Spray the air fryer basket with cooking spray and season the chicken bites with the salt, then place in the basket and air fry for 10 to 12 minutes or until crispy.
3. While the chicken bites cook, pour the hot sauce into a large bowl.
4. Remove the bites and add to the sauce bowl, tossing to coat. Serve warm.

Courgette and Potato Tots

Prep time: 5 minutes | Cook time: 20 minutes | Serves 4

1 large courgette, grated
1 medium baked potato, skin removed and mashed
20 g shredded Cheddar cheese

1 large egg, beaten
½ tsp. salt
Cooking spray

1. Preheat the air fryer to 200ºC.
2. Wrap the grated courgette in a paper towel and squeeze out any excess liquid, then combine the courgette, baked potato, shredded Cheddar cheese, egg, and salt in a large bowl.
3. Spray a baking dish with cooking spray, then place individual tbsps. of the courgette mixture in the dish and air fry for 10 minutes. Repeat this process with the remaining mixture.
4. Remove the tots and allow to cool on a wire rack for 5 minutes before serving.

Crispy Cajun Dill Pickle Chips

Prep time: 5 minutes | Cook time: 10 minutes | Makes 16 slices

30 g plain flour
60 g panko bread crumbs
1 large egg, beaten
2 tsps. Cajun seasoning
2 large dill pickles, sliced into 8 rounds each
Cooking spray

1. Preheat the air fryer to 200ºC.
2. Place the plain flour, panko bread crumbs, and egg into 3 separate shallow bowls, then stir the Cajun seasoning into the flour.
3. Dredge each pickle chip in the flour mixture, then the egg, and finally the bread crumbs. Shake off any excess, then place each coated pickle chip on a plate.
4. Spritz the air fryer basket with cooking spray, then place 8 pickle chips in the basket and air fry for 5 minutes, or until crispy and golden brown. Repeat this process with the remaining pickle chips.
5. Remove the chips and allow to slightly cool on a wire rack before serving.

Hasselback Potatoes

Prep time: 5 minutes | Cook time: 50 minutes | Serves 4

4 russet potatoes, peeled
Salt and freshly ground black pepper, to taste

22 g grated Parmesan cheese
Cooking spray

1. Preheat the air fryer to 200ºC.
2. Spray the air fryer basket lightly with cooking spray.
3. Make thin parallel cuts into each potato, ¼ cm to ½ cm apart, stopping at about ½ of the way through. The potato needs to stay intact along the bottom.
4. Spray the potatoes with cooking spray and use the hands or a silicone brush to completely coat the potatoes lightly in oil.
5. Put the potatoes, sliced side up, in the air fryer basket in a single layer. Leave a little room between each potato. Sprinkle the potatoes lightly with salt and black pepper.
6. Air fry for 20 minutes. Reposition the potatoes and spritz lightly with cooking spray again. Air fry until the potatoes are fork-tender and crispy and browned, another 20 to 30 minutes.
7. Sprinkle the potatoes with Parmesan cheese and serve.

Spinach and Crab Meat Cups

Prep time: 10 minutes | Cook time: 10 minutes | Makes 30 cups

1 (170-g) can crab meat, drained
20 g frozen spinach, thawed, drained, and chopped
1 clove garlic, minced
45 g grated Parmesan cheese
3 tbsps. plain yogurt

¼ tsp. lemon juice
½ tsp. Worcestershire sauce
30 mini frozen phyllo shells, thawed
Cooking spray

1. Preheat the air fryer to 200ºC.
2. Remove any bits of shell that might remain in the crab meat.
3. Mix the crab meat, spinach, garlic, and cheese together.
4. Stir in the yogurt, lemon juice, and Worcestershire sauce and mix well.
5. Spoon a tsp. of filling into each phyllo shell.
6. Spray the air fryer basket with cooking spray and arrange half the shells in the basket. Air fry for 5 minutes. Repeat with the remaining shells.
7. Serve immediately.

Cheesy Steak Fries

Prep time: 5 minutes | Cook time: 20 minutes | Serves 5

1 (794-g) bag frozen steak fries
Cooking spray
Salt and pepper, to taste

120 ml beef gravy
100 g shredded Mozzarella cheese
2 spring onions, green parts only, chopped

1. Preheat the air fryer to 200ºC.
2. Place the frozen steak fries in the air fryer. Air fry for 10 minutes. Shake the basket and spritz the fries with cooking spray. Sprinkle with salt and pepper. Air fry for an additional 8 minutes.
3. Pour the beef gravy into a medium, microwave-safe bowl. Microwave for 30 seconds, or until the gravy is warm.
4. Sprinkle the fries with the cheese. Air fry for an additional 2 minutes, until the cheese is melted.
5. Transfer the fries to a serving dish. Drizzle the fries with gravy and sprinkle the spring onions on top for a green garnish. Serve.

Cajun Courgette Chips

Prep time: 5 minutes | Cook time: 15 to 16 minutes | Serves 4

2 large courgettes, cut into ¼-cm-thick slices
2 tsps. Cajun seasoning

Cooking spray

1. Preheat the air fryer to 190ºC.
2. Spray the air fryer basket lightly with cooking spray.
3. Put the courgette slices in a medium bowl and spray them generously with cooking spray.
4. Sprinkle the Cajun seasoning over the courgette and stir to make sure they are evenly coated with oil and seasoning.
5. Place the slices in a single layer in the air fryer basket, making sure not to overcrowd. You will need to cook these in several batches.
6. Air fry for 8 minutes. Flip the slices over and air fry for an additional 7 to 8 minutes, or until they are as crisp and brown as you prefer.
7. Serve immediately.

Chapter 8 Desserts

Cheesecake

Prep time: 10 minutes | Cook time: 20 minutes | Serves 8

100 g crushed digestive biscuits
3 tbsps. softened butter
1½ (227-g) packages cream cheese, softened
70 g sugar
2 eggs
1 tbsp. flour
1 tsp. vanilla
60 ml chocolate syrup

1. For the crust, combine the crushed biscuits and butter in a small bowl and mix well. Press into the bottom of a baking dish and put in the freezer to set.
2. For the filling, combine the cream cheese and sugar in a medium bowl and mix well. Beat in the eggs, one at a time. Add the flour and vanilla.
3. Preheat the air fryer to 230ºC.
4. Remove ⅔ cup of the filling to a small bowl and stir in the chocolate syrup until combined.
5. Pour the vanilla filling into the dish with the crust. Drop the chocolate filling over the vanilla filling by the spoonful. With a clean butter knife, stir the fillings in a zigzag pattern to marbleize them.
6. Bake for 20 minutes or until the cheesecake is just set.
7. Cool on a wire rack for 1 hour, then chill in the refrigerator until the cheesecake is firm.
8. Serve immediately.

Orange Cake

Prep time: 10 minutes | Cook time: 23 minutes | Serves 8

Nonstick baking spray with flour
155 g plain flour
55 g yellow cornmeal
150 g white sugar
1 tsp. baking soda
60 ml safflower oil
300 ml orange juice, divided
1 tsp. vanilla
32 g icing sugar

1. Preheat the air fryer to 180ºC.
2. Spray a baking dish with nonstick spray and set aside.
3. In a medium bowl, combine the flour, cornmeal, sugar, baking soda, safflower oil, 240 ml of the orange juice, and vanilla, and mix well.
4. Pour the batter into the baking dish and place in the air fryer. Bake for 23 minutes or until a toothpick inserted in the centre of the cake comes out clean.
5. Remove the cake from the basket and place on a cooling rack. Using a toothpick, make about 20 holes in the cake.
6. In a small bowl, combine remaining 60 ml of orange juice and the icing sugar and stir well. Drizzle this mixture over the hot cake slowly so the cake absorbs it.
7. Cool completely, then cut into wedges to serve.

Curry Peaches, Pears, and Plums

Prep time: 5 minutes | Cook time: 5 minutes | Serves 6 to 8

2 peaches
2 firm pears
2 plums
2 tbsps. melted butter
1 tbsp. honey
2 to 3 tsps. curry powder

1. Preheat the air fryer to 160ºC.
2. Cut the peaches in half, remove the pits, and cut each half in half again. Cut the pears in half, core them, and remove the stem. Cut each half in half again. Do the same with the plums.
3. Spread a large sheet of heavy-duty foil on the work surface. Arrange the fruit on the foil and drizzle with the butter and honey. Sprinkle with the curry powder.
4. Wrap the fruit in the foil, making sure to leave some air space in the packet.
5. Put the foil package in the basket and bake for 5 to 8 minutes, shaking the basket once during the cooking time, until the fruit is soft.
6. Serve immediately.

Bacon and Broccoli Bread Pudding

Prep time: 15 minutes | Cook time: 48 minutes | Serves 2 to 4

227 g thick cut bacon, cut into ½ -cm pieces
200 g brioche bread, cut into 1-cm cubes
2 tbsps. butter, melted
3 eggs
240 ml milk
½ tsp. salt
Freshly ground black pepper, to taste
70 g frozen broccoli florets, thawed and chopped
125 g grated Swiss cheese

1. Preheat the air fryer to 200ºC.
2. Air fry the bacon for 8 minutes until crispy, shaking the basket a few times to help it air fry evenly. Remove the bacon and set it aside on a paper towel.
3. Air fry the brioche bread cubes for 2 minutes to dry and toast lightly.
4. Butter a cake pan. Combine all the ingredients in a large bowl and toss well. Transfer the mixture to the buttered cake pan, cover with aluminum foil and refrigerate the bread pudding overnight, or for at least 8 hours.
5. Remove the cake pan from the refrigerator an hour before you plan to bake and let it sit on the countertop to come to room temperature.
6. Preheat the air fryer to 166ºC. Transfer the covered cake pan to the basket of the air fryer, lowering the pan into the basket. Fold the ends of the aluminum foil over the top of the pan before returning the basket to the air fryer.
7. Air fry for 20 minutes. Remove the foil and air fry for an additional 20 minutes. If the top browns a little too much before the custard has set, simply return the foil to the pan. The bread pudding has cooked through when a skewer inserted into the centre comes out clean.
8. Serve warm.

Easy Mac & Cheese

Prep time: 10 minutes | Cook time: 10 minutes | Serves 2

230 g cooked macaroni
85 g grated Cheddar cheese
120 ml warm milk

Salt and ground black pepper, to taste
1 tbsp. grated Parmesan cheese

1. Preheat the air fryer to 180ºC.
2. In a baking dish, mix all the ingredients, except for Parmesan.
3. Put the dish inside the air fryer and bake for 10 minutes.
4. Add the Parmesan cheese on top and serve.

Black Forest Pies

Prep time: 10 minutes | Cook time: 15 minutes | Serves 6

3 tbsps. milk or dark chocolate chips
2 tbsps. thick, hot fudge sauce
2 tbsps. chopped dried cherries
1 (20-by-30-cm) sheet frozen puff pastry, thawed

1 egg white, beaten
2 tbsps. sugar
½ tsp. cinnamon

1. Preheat the air fryer to 180ºC.
2. In a small bowl, combine the chocolate chips, fudge sauce, and dried cherries.
3. Roll out the puff pastry on a floured surface. Cut into 6 squares with a sharp knife.
4. Divide the chocolate chip mixture into the centre of each puff pastry square. Fold the squares in half to make triangles. Firmly press the edges with the tines of a fork to seal.
5. Brush the triangles on all sides sparingly with the beaten egg white. Sprinkle the tops with sugar and cinnamon.
6. Put in the air fryer basket and bake for 15 minutes or until the triangles are golden brown. The filling will be hot, so cool for at least 20 minutes before serving.

Apple, Peach and Cranberry Crisp

Prep time: 10 minutes | Cook time: 12 minutes | Serves 8

1 apple, peeled and chopped
2 peaches, peeled and chopped
43 g dried cranberries
2 tbsps. honey
70 g brown sugar
30 g flour
80 g oats
3 tbsps. softened butter

1. Preheat the air fryer to 190ºC.
2. In a baking dish, combine the apple, peaches, cranberries, and honey, and mix well.
3. In a medium bowl, combine the brown sugar, flour, oats, and butter, and mix until crumbly. Sprinkle this mixture over the fruit in the dish.
4. Bake for 10 to 12 minutes or until the fruit is bubbly and the topping is golden brown. Serve warm.

Rich Chocolate Cookie

Prep time: 10 minutes | Cook time: 9 minutes | Serves 4

Nonstick baking spray with flour
3 tbsps. softened butter
73 g plus 1 tbsp. brown sugar
1 egg yolk
62 g flour
2 tbsps. ground white chocolate
¼ tsp. baking soda
½ tsp. vanilla
60 g chocolate chips

1. Preheat the air fryer to 180ºC.
2. In a medium bowl, beat the butter and brown sugar together until fluffy. Stir in the egg yolk.
3. Add the flour, white chocolate, baking soda, and vanilla, and mix well. Stir in the chocolate chips.
4. Line a baking dish with parchment paper. Spray the parchment paper with nonstick baking spray with flour.
5. Spread the batter into the prepared dish, leaving a 1-cm border on all sides.
6. Bake for about 9 minutes or until the cookie is light brown and just barely set.
7. Remove the baking dish from the air fryer and let cool for 10 minutes. Remove the cookie from the baking dish, remove the parchment paper, and let cool on a wire rack.
8. Serve immediately.

Chocolate and Peanut Butter Lava Cupcakes

Prep time: 10 minutes | Cook time: 10 to 13 minutes | Serves 8

Nonstick baking spray with flour
170 g chocolate cake mix
1 egg
1 egg yolk
60 ml safflower oil

60 ml hot water
80 g sour cream
3 tbsps. peanut butter
1 tbsp. powdered sugar

1. Preheat the air fryer to 180ºC.
2. Double up 16 foil muffin cups to make 8 cups. Spray each lightly with nonstick spray; set aside.
3. In a medium bowl, combine the cake mix, egg, egg yolk, safflower oil, water, and sour cream, and beat until combined.
4. In a small bowl, combine the peanut butter and powdered sugar and mix well. Form this mixture into 8 balls.
5. Spoon about ¼ cup of the chocolate batter into each muffin cup and top with a peanut butter ball. Spoon remaining batter on top of the peanut butter balls to cover them.
6. Arrange the cups in the air fryer basket, leaving some space between each. Bake for 10 to 13 minutes or until the tops look dry and set.
7. Let the cupcakes cool for about 10 minutes, then serve warm.

Mushroom and Pepper Pizza Squares

Prep time: 10 minutes | Cook time: 10 minutes | Serves 10

1 pizza dough, cut into squares
75 g chopped oyster mushrooms
1 shallot, chopped

¼ red pepper, chopped
2 tbsps. parsley
Salt and ground black pepper, to taste

1. Preheat the air fryer to 200ºC.
2. In a bowl, combine the oyster mushrooms, shallot, pepper and parsley. Sprinkle some salt and pepper as desired.
3. Spread this mixture on top of the pizza squares.
4. Bake in the air fryer for 10 minutes.
5. Serve warm.

Lemony Blackberry Crisp

Prep time: 5 minutes | Cook time: 20 minutes | Serves 1

2 tbsps. lemon juice
8 g powdered sweetener
¼ tsp. xantham gum

320 g blackberries
100 g crunchy granola

1. Preheat the air fryer to 180ºC.
2. In a bowl, combine the lemon juice, sweetener, xantham gum, and blackberries. Transfer to a round baking dish and cover with aluminum foil.
3. Put the dish in the air fryer and bake for 12 minutes.
4. Take care when removing the dish from the air fryer. Give the blackberries a stir and top with the granola.
5. Return the dish to the air fryer and bake for an additional 3 minutes, this time at 160ºC. Serve once the granola has turned brown and enjoy.

Chapter 9 Fast and Easy Everyday Favorites

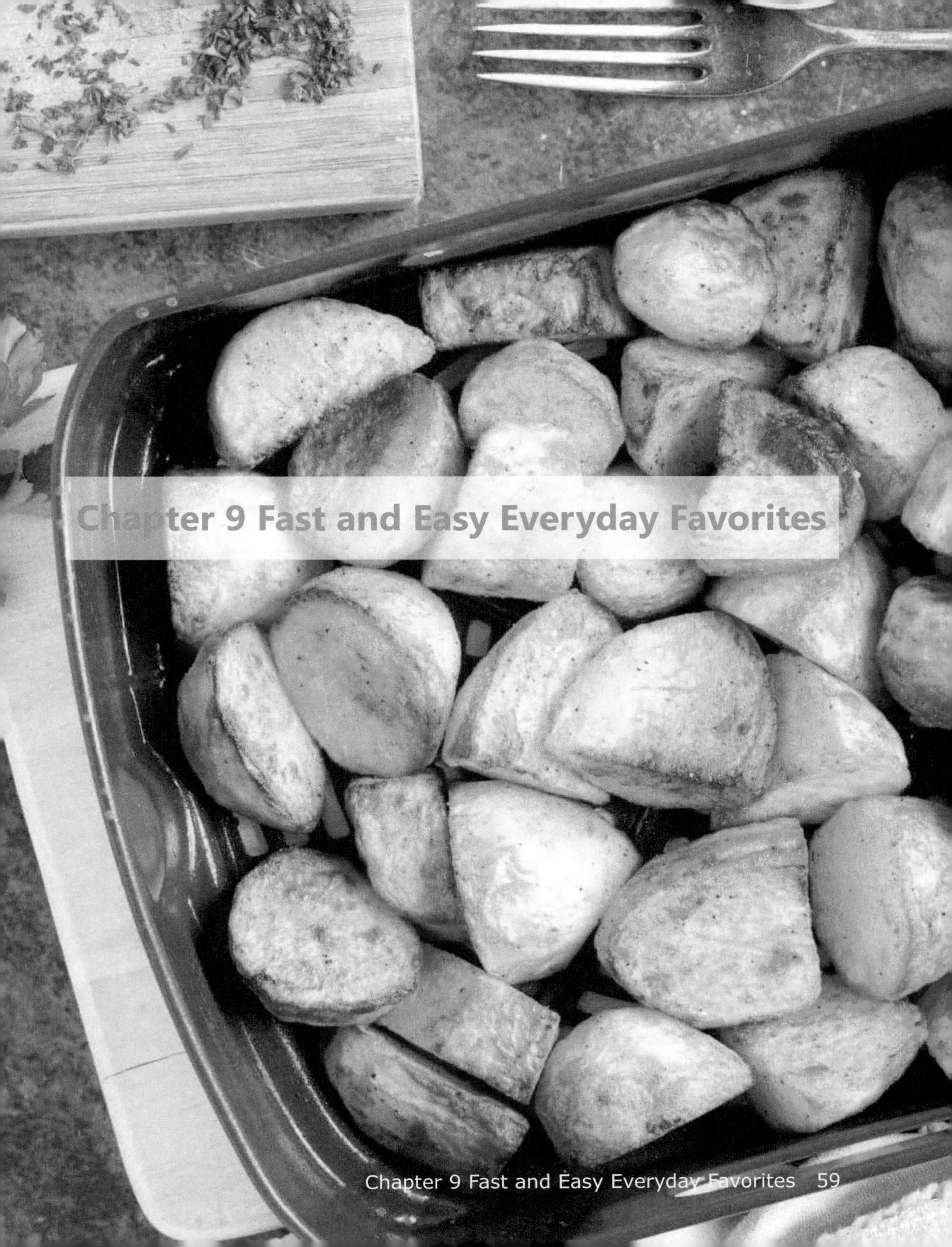

Fast and Easy Tortilla Chips

Prep time: 5 minutes | Cook time: 3 minutes | Serves 2

8 corn tortillas
1 tbsp. olive oil
Salt, to taste

1. Preheat the air fryer to 200ºC.
2. Slice the corn tortillas into triangles. Coat with a light brushing of olive oil.
3. Put the tortilla pieces in the air fryer basket and air fry for 3 minutes. You may need to do this in batches.
4. Season with salt before serving.

Mexican Pork Chops

Prep time: 5 minutes | Cook time: 15 minutes | Serves 2

¼ tsp. dried oregano
1½ tsps. taco seasoning mix
2 (113-g) boneless pork chops
2 tbsps. unsalted butter, divided

1. Preheat the air fryer to 200ºC.
2. Combine the dried oregano and taco seasoning in a small bowl and rub the mixture into the pork chops. Brush the chops with 1 tbsp. butter.
3. In the air fryer, air fry the chops for 15 minutes, turning them over halfway through to air fry on the other side.
4. When the chops are a brown colour, check the internal temperature has reached 65ºC and remove from the air fryer. Serve with a garnish of remaining butter.

Classic Mexican Street Corn

Prep time: 5 minutes | Cook time: 7 minutes | Serves 4

4 medium ears corn, husked
Cooking spray
2 tbsps. mayonnaise
1 tbsp. fresh lime juice
½ tsp. ancho chili powder
¼ tsp. salt
57 g crumbled Cotija or Feta cheese
2 tbsps. chopped fresh coriander

1. Preheat the air fryer to 190ºC.
2. Spritz the corn with cooking spray. Working in batches, arrange the ears of corn in the air fryer basket in a single layer. Air fry for about 7 minutes, flipping halfway, until the kernels are tender when pierced with a paring knife. When cool enough to handle, cut the corn kernels off the cob.
3. In a large bowl, mix together mayonnaise, lime juice, ancho powder, and salt. Add the corn kernels and mix to combine. Transfer to a serving dish and top with the Cotija and coriander. Serve immediately.

Herb-Roasted Veggies

Prep time: 10 minutes | Cook time: 14 to 18 minutes | Serves 4

1 red pepper, sliced
1 (227-g) package sliced mushrooms
125 g green beans, cut into 4-cm pieces
25 g diced red onion

3 garlic cloves, sliced
1 tsp. olive oil
½ tsp. dried basil
½ tsp. dried tarragon

1. Preheat the air fryer to 180ºC.
2. In a medium bowl, mix the red pepper, mushrooms, green beans, red onion, and garlic. Drizzle with the olive oil. Toss to coat.
3. Add the herbs and toss again.
4. Place the vegetables in the air fryer basket. Roast for 14 to 18 minutes, or until tender. Serve immediately.

Cheesy Jalapeño Poppers

Prep time: 5 minutes | Cook time: 10 minutes | Serves 4

8 jalapeño peppers
112 g whipped cream cheese

20 g shredded Cheddar cheese

1. Preheat the air fryer to 180ºC.
2. Use a paring knife to carefully cut off the jalapeño tops, then scoop out the ribs and seeds. Set aside.
3. In a medium bowl, combine the whipped cream cheese and shredded Cheddar cheese. Place the mixture in a sealable plastic bag, and using a pair of scissors, cut off one corner from the bag. Gently squeeze some cream cheese mixture into each pepper until almost full.
4. Place a piece of parchment paper on the bottom of the air fryer basket and place the poppers on top, distributing evenly. Air fry for 10 minutes.
5. Allow the poppers to cool for 5 to 10 minutes before serving.

Bacon-Wrapped Jalapeño Poppers

Prep time: 5 minutes | Cook time: 12 minutes | Serves 6

6 large jalapeños
113 g ⅓-less-fat cream cheese
30 g shredded reduced-fat sharp Cheddar cheese
2 spring onions, green tops only, sliced
6 slices centre-cut bacon, halved

1. Preheat the air fryer to 160ºC.
2. Wearing rubber gloves, halve the jalapeños lengthwise to make 12 pieces. Scoop out the seeds and membranes and discard.
3. In a medium bowl, combine the cream cheese, Cheddar, and spring onions. Using a small spoon or spatula, fill the jalapeños with the cream cheese filling. Wrap a bacon strip around each pepper and secure with a toothpick.
4. Working in batches, place the stuffed peppers in a single layer in the air fryer basket. Bake for about 12 minutes, until the peppers are tender, the bacon is browned and crisp, and the cheese is melted.
5. Serve warm.

Easy Devils on Horseback

Prep time: 5 minutes | Cook time: 7 minutes | Serves 12

24 petite pitted prunes (128 g)
55 g crumbled blue cheese, divided

8 slices centre-cut bacon, cut crosswise into thirds

1. Preheat the air fryer to 200ºC.
2. Halve the prunes lengthwise, but don't cut them all the way through. Place ½ tsp. of cheese in the centre of each prune. Wrap a piece of bacon around each prune and secure the bacon with a toothpick.
3. Working in batches, arrange a single layer of the prunes in the air fryer basket. Air fry for about 7 minutes, flipping halfway, until the bacon is cooked through and crisp.
4. Let cool slightly and serve warm.

Green Curry Prawn

Prep time: 15 minutes | Cook time: 5 minutes | Serves 4

1 to 2 tbsps. Thai green curry paste
2 tbsps. coconut oil, melted
1 tbsp. half-and-half or coconut milk
1 tsp. fish sauce
1 tsp. soy sauce

1 tsp. minced fresh ginger
1 clove garlic, minced
454 g jumbo raw prawns, peeled and deveined
15 g chopped fresh Thai basil or sweet basil
15 g chopped fresh coriander

1. In a baking dish, combine the curry paste, coconut oil, half-and-half, fish sauce, soy sauce, ginger, and garlic. Whisk until well combined.
2. Add the prawns and toss until well coated. Marinate at room temperature for 15 to 30 minutes.
3. Preheat the air fryer to 200ºC.
4. Place the baking dish in the air fryer basket. Air fry for 5 minutes, stirring halfway through the cooking time.
5. Transfer the prawns to a serving bowl or platter. Garnish with the basil and coriander. Serve immediately.

Scalloped Veggie Mix

Prep time: 10 minutes | Cook time: 15 minutes | Serves 4

1 Yukon Gold potato, thinly sliced
1 small sweet potato, peeled and thinly sliced
1 medium carrot, thinly sliced
20 g minced onion

3 garlic cloves, minced
180 ml low fat milk
2 tbsps. cornflour
½ tsp. dried thyme

1. Preheat the air fryer to 190ºC.
2. In a baking dish, layer the potato, sweet potato, carrot, onion, and garlic.
3. In a small bowl, whisk the milk, cornflour, and thyme until blended. Pour the milk mixture evenly over the vegetables in the dish.
4. Bake for 15 minutes. Check the casserole—it should be golden brown on top, and the vegetables should be tender.
5. Serve immediately.

Indian Masala Omelet

Prep time: 10 minutes | Cook time: 12 minutes | Serves 2

4 large eggs
30 g diced onion
80 g diced tomato
15 g chopped fresh coriander
1 jalapeño, deseeded and finely chopped
½ tsp. ground turmeric
½ tsp. salt
½ tsp. cayenne pepper
Olive oil, for greasing the pan

1. Preheat the air fryer to 120ºC. Generously grease a 3-cup Bundt pan.
2. In a large bowl, beat the eggs. Stir in the onion, tomato, coriander, jalapeño, turmeric, salt, and cayenne.
3. Pour the egg mixture into the prepared pan. Place the pan in the air fryer basket. Bake for 12 minutes, or until the eggs are cooked through. Carefully unmold and cut the omelet into four pieces.
4. Serve immediately.

Traditional Queso Fundido

Prep time: 10 minutes | Cook time: 25 minutes | Serves 4

113 g fresh Mexican chorizo, casings removed
1 medium onion, chopped
3 cloves garlic, minced
180 g chopped tomato
2 jalapeños, deseeded and diced
2 tsps. ground cumin
220 g shredded Oaxaca or Mozzarella cheese
60 ml half-and-half
Celery sticks or tortilla chips, for serving

1. Preheat the air fryer to 200ºC.
2. In a baking pan, combine the chorizo, onion, garlic, tomato, jalapeños, and cumin. Stir to combine.
3. Place the pan in the air fryer basket. Air fry for 15 minutes, or until the sausage is cooked, stirring halfway through the cooking time to break up the sausage.
4. Add the cheese and half-and-half; stir to combine. Air fry for 10 minutes, or until the cheese has melted.
5. Serve with celery sticks or tortilla chips.

Appendix 1: Measurement Conversion Chart

WEIGHT EQUIVALENTS

METRIC	US STANDARD	US STANDARD (OUNCES)
15 g	1 tablespoon	1/2 ounce
30 g	1/8 cup	1 ounce
60 g	1/4 cup	2 ounces
115 g	1/2 cup	4 ounces
170 g	3/4 cup	6 ounces
225 g	1 cup	8 ounces
450 g	2 cups	16 ounces
900 g	4 cups	2 pounds

VOLUME EQUIVALENTS

METRIC	US STANDARD	US STANDARD (OUNCES)
15 ml	1 tablespoon	1/2 fl.oz.
30 ml	2 tablespoons	1 fl.oz.
60 ml	1/4 cup	2 fl.oz.
125 ml	1/2 cup	4 fl.oz.
180 ml	3/4 cup	6 fl.oz.
250 ml	1 cup	8 fl.oz.
500 ml	2 cups	16 fl.oz.
1000 ml	4 cups	1 quart

TEMPERATURES EQUIVALENTS

CELSIUS (C)	FAHRENHEIT (F) (APPROXIMATE)
120 °C	250 °F
135 °C	275 °F
150 °C	300 °F
160 °C	325 °F
175 °C	350 °F
190 °C	375 °F
205 °C	400 °F
220 °C	425 °F
230 °C	450 °F
245°C	475 °F
260 °C	500 °F

LENGTH EQUIVALENTS

METRIC	IMPERIAL
3 mm	1/8 inch
6 mm	1/4 inch
1 cm	1/2 inch
2.5 cm	1 inch
3 cm	1 1/4 inches
5 cm	2 inches
10 cm	4 inches
15 cm	6 inches
20 cm	8 inches

Appendix 2: Air Fryer Time Table

Vegetable

Item	Temp(°F)	Time (mins)	Item	Temp(°F)	Time (mins)
Asparagus (sliced 2-cm)	205°C	5	Mushrooms (sliced ½-cm)	205°C	5
Aubergine (4-cm cubes)	205°C	15	Onions (pearl)	205°C	10
Beetroots (whole)	205°C	40	Parsnips (1-cm chunks)	195°C	15
Broccoli (florets)	205°C	6	Peppers (2-cm chunks)	205°C	15
Brussels Sprouts (halved)	195°C	15	Potatoes (small baby, 650 g)	205°C	14
Carrots (sliced 1-cm)	195°C	15	Potatoes (2-cm chunks)	205°C	12
Cauliflower (florets)	205°C	12	Potatoes (baked whole)	205°C	40
Corn on the cob	200°C	6	Runner Beans	205°C	5
Courgette (1-cm sticks)	205°C	12	Sweet Potato (baked)	195°C	30 to 35
Fennel (quartered)	190°C	15	Tomatoes (cherry)	205°C	4
Kale leaves	120°C	12	Tomatoes (halves)	180°C	10

Chicken

Item	Temp(°F)	Time (mins)	Item	Temp(°F)	Time (mins)
Breasts, bone in (550 g)	190°C	24	Legs, bone in (800 g)	195°C	30
Breasts, boneless (150 g)	195°C	14	Wings (900 g)	205°C	12
Drumsticks (1.1 kg)	190°C	20	Game Hen (halved – 900 g)	200°C	20
Thighs, bone in (900 g)	195°C	22	Whole Chicken (3 kg)	185°C	75
Thighs, boneless (700 g)	195°C	20	Tenders	185°C	8 to 10

Beef

Item	Temp(°F)	Time (mins)	Item	Temp(°F)	Time (mins)
Burger (120 g)	190°C	16 to 20	Meatballs (7-cm)	195°C	10
Filet Mignon (250 g)	205°C	18-20	Ribeye, bone in (2-cm, 250 g)	205°C	12 to 15
Flank Steak (700 g)	205°C	13	Sirloin steaks (2-cm, 350 g)	205°C	10 to 14
London Broil (900 g)	205°C	20 to 28	Beef Eye Round Roast (1.8 kg)	200°C	45 to 55
Meatballs (2-cm)	195°C	7			

Pork and Lamb

Item	Temp(°F)	Time (mins)	Item	Temp(°F)	Time (mins)
Loin (900 g)	185°C	55	Bacon (thick cut)	205°C	6 to 10
Pork Chops, bone in (2-cm, 200 g)	205°C	13	Sausages	195°C	15
Tenderloin (450 g)	190°C	15	Lamb Loin Chops (2-cm thick)	205°C	8 to 12
Bacon (regular)	205°C	5 to 7	Rack of lamb (600-1000 g)	195°C	23

Fish and Seafood

Item	Temp(°F)	Time (mins)	Item	Temp(°F)	Time (mins)
Calamari (250 g)	205°C	5	Tuna steak	205°C	7 to 10
Fish Fillet (2-cm, 250 g)	205°C	12	Scallops	205°C	5 to 7
Salmon, fillet (200 g)	195°C	12-14	Prawn	205°C	5
Swordfish steak	205°C	10			

Frozen Foods

Item	Temp(°F)	Time (mins)	Item	Temp(°F)	Time (mins)
Onion Rings (350 g)	205°C	9	Fish Sticks (300 g)	205°C	11
Thin Chips (550 g)	205°C	13	Fish Fillets (1-cm, 300 g)	205°C	15
Thick Chips (500 g)	205°C	20	Chicken Nuggets (350 g)	205°C	10
Mozzarella Sticks (300 g)	205°C	8	Breaded Prawn	205°C	9
Pot Stickers (300 g)	205°C	8			

Appendix 3: 365 Days Meal Plan

Day 1-5	Fast Coffee Donuts	Lush Summer Rolls	Sweet-and-Sour Drumsticks	Country Prawn	Greek Lamb Rack
Day 6-10	Crispy Cod Cakes with Salad Greens	Scalloped Veggie Mix	Crispy Cajun Dill Pickle Chips	Lush Summer Rolls	Fig, Chickpea, and Rocket Salad
Day 11-15	Corn Pakodas	Cashew Stuffed Mushrooms	Traditional Queso Fundido	Celery Chicken	Crisp Paprika Chicken Drumsticks
Day 16-20	Soufflé	Chicken-Lettuce Wraps	Lush Summer Rolls	Easy Mac & Cheese	Crisp Paprika Chicken Drumsticks
Day 21-25	Fig, Chickpea, and Rocket Salad	Cheesy Macaroni Balls	Mushroom and Pepper Pizza Squares	Blackened Chicken Breasts	Classic Mexican Street Corn
Day 26-30	Cheesy Jalapeño Poppers	Bacon Hot Dogs	Spinach and Crab Meat Cups	Kale and Potato Nuggets	Hasselback Potatoes
Day 31-35	Potato Cheese Crusted Chicken	Soufflé	Cheesy Jalapeño Poppers	Blackened Chicken Breasts	Cheese Crusted Chops
Day 36-40	Lush Summer Rolls	Easy Mac & Cheese	Pork Chop Stir Fry	Potato Bread Rolls	Marinated Pork Tenderloin
Day 41-45	Cheesy Steak Fries	Italian Lamb Chops with Avocado Mayo	Traditional Queso Fundido	Mushroom and Pepper Pizza Squares	Corn Pakodas
Day 40-50	Cajun-Style Salmon Burgers	Marinated Pork Tenderloin	Crispy Cod Cakes with Salad Greens	Herbed Pita Chips	Homemade Fish Sticks
Day 51-55	Rice and Aubergine Bowl	Simple Salmon Bites	Cheesecake	Crispy Cod Cakes with Salad Greens	Chicken-Lettuce Wraps
Day 56-60	Marinated Pork Tenderloin	Crisp Paprika Chicken Drumsticks	Pork Chop Stir Fry	Crisp Paprika Chicken Drumsticks	Crumbed Golden Filet Mignon
Day 61-65	Easy Mac & Cheese	Air Fried Beef Ribs	Super Vegetable Burger	Italian Lamb Chops with Avocado Mayo	Spicy Chicken Bites
Day 66-70	Potato Cheese Crusted Chicken	Pigs in a Blanket	Cheesy Jalapeño Poppers	Cheesy Macaroni Balls	Homemade Fish Sticks
Day 71-75	Potato Bread Rolls	Avocado Buttered Flank Steak	Cheesy Steak Fries	Rice and Aubergine Bowl	Apple, Peach and Cranberry Crisp
Day 76-80	Cashew Stuffed Mushrooms	Spinach and Crab Meat Cups	Crispy Chicken Strips	Cheesecake	Celery Chicken
Day 81-85	Traditional Queso Fundido	Indian Masala Omelet	Black Forest Pies	Cheese Crusted Chops	Classic Mexican Street Corn
Day 86-90	Air Fryer Naked Chicken Tenders	Avocado Buttered Flank Steak	Mexican Pork Chops	Homemade Fish Sticks	Chicken-Lettuce Wraps
Day 91-95	Orange Cake	Bacon Hot Dogs	Hasselback Potatoes	Chocolate and Peanut Butter Lava Cupcakes	Italian Lamb Chops with Avocado Mayo
Day 96-100	Potato Bread Rolls	Cajun-Style Salmon Burgers	Piri-Piri Chicken Thighs	Crispy Cajun Dill Pickle Chips	Super Vegetable Burger

Day 101-105	Honey Rosemary Chicken	Indian Masala Omelet	Bacon and Broccoli Bread Pudding	Marinated Pork Tenderloin	Potato Cheese Crusted Chicken
Day 106-110	Orange Cake	Cheese Crusted Chops	Cornflakes Toast Sticks	Pigs in a Blanket	Air Fried Ribeye Steak
Day 111-115	Rice and Aubergine Bowl	Air Fryer Naked Chicken Tenders	Nutty Chicken Tenders	Avocado Buttered Flank Steak	Cashew Stuffed Mushrooms
Day 116-120	Blackened Chicken Breasts	Pork Chop Stir Fry	Mexican Pork Chops	Cheesy Macaroni Balls	Sweet Potatoes with Tofu
Day 121-125	Tuna Sliders	Corn Pakodas	Crispy Chicken Strips	Cheesy Steak Fries	Simple Salmon Bites
Day 126-130	Creamy Cinnamon Rolls	Italian Lamb Chops with Avocado Mayo	Chocolate and Peanut Butter Lava Cupcakes	Chicken Fried Steak	Crisp Paprika Chicken Drumsticks
Day 131-135	Sweet Potatoes with Tofu	Hasselback Potatoes	Bacon and Broccoli Bread Pudding	Soufflé	Cajun Courgette Chips
Day 136-140	Piri-Piri Chicken Thighs	Indian Masala Omelet	Super Vegetable Burger	Herbed Beef	Cheesecake
Day 141-145	Simple Pesto Gnocchi	Mushroom and Pepper Pizza Squares	Sesame Glazed Salmon	Classic Mexican Street Corn	Creamy Cinnamon Rolls
Day 146-150	Sweet-and-Sour Drumsticks	Crispy Cajun Dill Pickle Chips	Cornflakes Toast Sticks	Spinach and Crab Meat Cups	Crispy Mozzarella Sticks
Day 151-155	Honey Rosemary Chicken	Cajun-Style Salmon Burgers	Crispy Chicken Strips	Seasoned Breaded Prawn	Balsamic Brussels Sprouts
Day 156-160	Bacon and Broccoli Bread Pudding	Cajun Courgette Chips	Air Fried Ribeye Steak	Scalloped Veggie Mix	Crispy Cod Cakes with Salad Greens
Day 161-165	Tuna Sliders	Cornflakes Toast Sticks	Avocado Buttered Flank Steak	Greek Lamb Rack	Herbed Beef
Day 166-170	Mexican Pork Chops	Chicken Fried Steak	Balsamic Brussels Sprouts	Easy Devils on Horseback	Seasoned Breaded Prawn
Day 171-175	Sweet-and-Sour Drumsticks	Honey Rosemary Chicken	Chocolate and Peanut Butter Lava Cupcakes	Cajun-Style Fish Tacos	Fig, Chickpea, and Rocket Salad
Day 176-180	Celery Chicken	Pigs in a Blanket	Crispy Mozzarella Sticks	Simple Salmon Bites	Crispy Cajun Dill Pickle Chips
Day 181-185	Herbed Beef	Fast Coffee Donuts	Golden Avocado Tempura	Scalloped Veggie Mix	Air Fryer Naked Chicken Tenders
Day 186-190	Sweet Potatoes with Tofu	Spicy Chicken Bites	Easy Devils on Horseback	Tuna Sliders	Beef Loin with Thyme and Parsley
Day 191-195	Orange Cake	Dill Chicken Strips	Italian Lamb Chops with Avocado Mayo	Kale and Potato Nuggets	Air Fried Beef Ribs
Day 196-200	Fig, Chickpea, and Rocket Salad	Scalloped Veggie Mix	Nutty Chicken Tenders	Crumbed Golden Filet Mignon	Roasted Lemony Broccoli
Day 201-205	Herb-Roasted Veggies	Italian Lamb Chops with Avocado Mayo	Air Fried Ribeye Steak	Spinach Omelet	Curry Peaches, Pears, and Plums
Day 206-210	Chicken Fried Steak	Fast Coffee Donuts	Greek Lamb Pita Pockets	Sesame Glazed Salmon	Sriracha Golden Cauliflower

Day 211-215	Air Fried Beef Ribs	Sweet-and-Sour Drumsticks	Apple, Peach and Cranberry Crisp	Cajun Courgette Chips	Courgette and Potato Tots
Day 216-220	Balsamic Brussels Sprouts	Chocolate and Peanut Butter Lava Cupcakes	Easy Devils on Horseback	Cajun-Style Fish Tacos	Lemon Parmesan Chicken
Day 221-225	Simple Pesto Gnocchi	Lime-Chili Prawn Bowl	Crisp Paprika Chicken Drumsticks	Fast Coffee Donuts	Black Forest Pies
Day 226-230	Beef Chuck Cheeseburgers	Roasted Lemony Broccoli	Country Prawn	Green Curry Prawn	Blackened Prawn Tacos
Day 231-235	Bacon and Broccoli Bread Pudding	Fried Buffalo Chicken Taquitos	Dill Chicken Strips	Greek Lamb Rack	Simple Pesto Gnocchi
Day 236-240	Spanish Garlic Prawn	Rich Chocolate Cookie	Cheese Crusted Chops	Creamy Cinnamon Rolls	Cajun-Style Fish Tacos
Day 241-245	Spinach Omelet	Blackened Prawn Tacos	Crumbed Golden Filet Mignon	Crispy Mozzarella Sticks	Herbed Pita Chips
Day 246-250	Apple, Peach and Cranberry Crisp	Spicy Chicken Bites	Bacon-Wrapped Jalapeño Poppers	Greek Lamb Pita Pockets	Cheesy Bacon Quiche
Day 251-255	Spinach Omelet	Air Fried Olives	Chicken Satay with Peanut Sauce	Vegetable and Fish Tacos	Black Forest Pies
Day 256-260	Roasted Chicken Tenders with Veggies	Bacon-Wrapped Jalapeño Poppers	Green Curry Prawn	Sourdough Croutons	Beef Stuffed Peppers
Day 261-265	Cheese Crusted Chops	Lemon Parmesan Chicken	Courgette and Potato Tots	Sriracha Golden Cauliflower	Sesame Glazed Salmon
Day 266-270	Seasoned Breaded Prawn	Nutty Chicken Tenders	Rich Chocolate Cookie	Crumbed Golden Filet Mignon	Roasted Lemony Broccoli
Day 271-275	Apple, Peach and Cranberry Crisp	Spicy Orange Prawn	Honey Sriracha Chicken Wings	Ritzy Vegetable Frittata	Beef Chuck Cheeseburgers
Day 276-280	Country Prawn	Bacon Hot Dogs	Garlic-Lemon Tilapia	Herbed Pita Chips	Marinated Salmon Fillets
Day 281-285	Herb-Roasted Veggies	Italian Lamb Chops with Avocado Mayo	Blackened Prawn Tacos	Beef Loin with Thyme and Parsley	Dill Chicken Strips
Day 286-290	Cheesy Bacon Quiche	Lime-Chili Prawn Bowl	Sourdough Croutons	Beef Stuffed Peppers	Greek Lamb Rack
Day 291-295	Curry Peaches, Pears, and Plums	Israeli Chicken Schnitzel	Pork Medallions with Radicchio and Endive Salad	Roasted Chicken Tenders with Veggies	Spicy Orange Prawn
Day 296-300	Herb-Roasted Veggies	Cheese Crusted Chops	Fried Buffalo Chicken Taquitos	Vegetable and Fish Tacos	Chicken Satay with Peanut Sauce
Day 301-305	Courgette and Potato Tots	Fajita Chicken Strips	Rich Chocolate Cookie	Mini Quiche Cups	Bacon-Wrapped Jalapeño Poppers
Day 306-310	Piri-Piri Chicken Thighs	Fast and Easy Tortilla Chips	Kielbasa Sausage with Pierogies	Ritzy Vegetable Frittata	Marinated Salmon Fillets
Day 311-315	Marinated Salmon Fillets	Green Curry Prawn	Garlic-Lemon Tilapia	Beef Chuck Cheeseburgers	Lemon Parmesan Chicken
Day 316-320	Golden Avocado Tempura	Garlic-Lemon Tilapia	Fajita Chicken Strips	Lemony Blackberry Crisp	Spanish Garlic Prawn

Day 321-325	Beef Loin with Thyme and Parsley	Potatoes Lyonnaise	Spanish Garlic Prawn	Kale and Potato Nuggets	Spicy Orange Prawn
Day 326-330	Pork Medallions with Radicchio and Endive Salad	Nutty Chicken Tenders	Black Forest Pies	Roasted Chicken Tenders with Veggies	Lemony Blackberry Crisp
Day 331-335	Sourdough Croutons	Greek Lamb Pita Pockets	Lime-Chili Prawn Bowl	Air Fried Beef Ribs	Air Fried Olives
Day 336-340	Curry Peaches, Pears, and Plums	Chicken Satay with Peanut Sauce	Honey Sriracha Chicken Wings	Ritzy Vegetable Frittata	Herbed Pita Chips
Day 341-345	Kielbasa Sausage with Pierogies	Beef Stuffed Peppers	Potatoes Lyonnaise	Fast and Easy Tortilla Chips	Country Prawn
Day 346-350	Cheesy Bacon Quiche	Vegetable and Fish Tacos	Israeli Chicken Schnitzel	Pork Medallions with Radicchio and Endive Salad	Roasted Lemony Broccoli
Day 351-355	Fried Buffalo Chicken Taquitos	Lemony Blackberry Crisp	Fajita Chicken Strips	Mini Quiche Cups	Honey Sriracha Chicken Wings
Day 356-360	Kielbasa Sausage with Pierogies	Kale and Potato Nuggets	Air Fried Olives	Israeli Chicken Schnitzel	Potatoes Lyonnaise
Day 361-365	Fried Buffalo Chicken Taquitos	Mini Quiche Cups	Sriracha Golden Cauliflower	Fast and Easy Tortilla Chips	Golden Avocado Tempura

Appendix 4: Recipes Index

Dear Readers,

We are glad that you purchased this book, your opinion is very important to us. If you have any comments and suggestions on this cookbook, we sincerely invite you to send us an email for feedback.

With your participation, we will grow faster and better.

After receiving your email, we will upgrade the product according to your needs and give you an e-book of 50 recipes as a gift.

We are committed to continuous growth and progress, providing readers with cookbooks that help create a better kitchen life and a healthy body.

I wish you happy every day.

Company contact email: Healthrecipegroup@outlook.com

Printed in Great Britain
by Amazon